THE TURGENEV FAMILY

by

Mme V. Zhitova

London
The Harvill Press

Published in 1947
The Harvill Press Ltd.
23 *Lower Belgrave St., London.*

Printed in Great Britain
Crosskey Bros., Ltd.

The Turgenev Family

Translated by
A. S. MILLS

With an Introduction by
A. MEYENDORF

Contents

CONTENTS

Introduction

It is now about fifteen years since my stay in the house of some friends in Finland where, for the first time, I came across *The Turgenev Family* in a stray copy of *Vestnik Evropy** for November-December, 1884. I discussed the possibility of translating it with Mme. C. Zvegitsov, who had already tackled so difficult an author as Merejkowsky, and I saw that the deep impression which the story had produced on me was shared by her and by others. True, the book throws a melancholy light on a great country's not very remote past. But there is in it a fascination and a power—the power of a tragedy whose characters are "convincing" in the sense used, I believe, by literary critics to denote types which can be not only imagined but met in real life, and recognised not only by the psychiatrist but by the ordinary observer.

It is true that the modern equivalents of these types cannot be identical, since the story is about events which took place in Central Russia at the time of serfdom, between 1834 and 1851. But this does not mean that the tale has lost all its actuality, any more than *Uncle Tom's Cabin*, which appeared in 1852, twelve years before the abolition of slavery in the United States. We can still recognise those among us who would have taken part in the five years' struggle in America, and fought either with the South for its own solution of the problem, or with the North for immediate emancipation. We can even visualise the refined and mildly reproachful humanitarian, St. Clare, depicted by Mrs. Beecher Stowe as a passive sufferer under the coarse conditions of a slave-driving household headed by his capricious wife.

*Vestnik Yevropy (THE EUROPEAN MESSENGER) a Russian literary review.

The reader may draw certain parallels between the American and the Russian household. But *The Turgenev Family* is not an imaginary story conceived as a means of promoting a good cause; nor does it purport to describe Russian country life prior to the abolition of serfdom. If the writer had a " case " it was to give a true portrait of Turgenev's mother in contrast to what was believed about her in a gossiping world. As a first hand and unselfconscious account of the society in which she lived, the book is, to my mind, of outstanding merit.

*   *   *   *

In 1834, when the reminiscences begin, Mme. Turgenev's son, Ivan, was only sixteen. In the following year, as a student at St. Petersburg University, he had the opportunity of observing the peculiar display made by Gogol as professor of history (his appointment, like that of Schiller, was inspired by charitable motives). He also met Zhukovsky, the poet and translator of French, German and English masterpieces, an old acquaintance of his mother's, who was at that time tutor to the heir apparent, the future Tsar Liberator, Alexander II.

Having graduated at the Faculty of Philology in 1837, writes Turgenev, I went to Berlin as to a finishing school. I was convinced that in Russia one could obtain no more than a preliminary knowledge, but that real knowledge—its very source—was in the West. Among the University teachers of those days there was not one who could have shaken me in that conviction. Indeed, it was what they thought themselves; the Ministry was of the same opinion, and Count Uvavrov, Minister of Education, arranged for young men to be sent to German universities at the expense of the Treasury. In Berlin I spent two years.

Among the Russian students there I can mention . . .
N. Stankovitch, Granovsky, Frolov and . . . M.
Bakunin, of later fame. We may add of international
fame, and the former three became leaders of liberal
thought in Russia.

Turgenev read "philosophy, classics and history, and,
with particular zeal, studied Hegel's philosophy under
Weber." The reputation of Hegel in this country is at a
very low ebb, and even people who ought to know better
quote against him his view of the Prussian Monarchy,
though his foible for it was no greater than Macaulay's
for the social and economic conditions of his time. For
the Russians, and not only for them, Hegel's philosophy
stood for the inevitability of movement, and as such, it
served their aspirations towards progress.

Turgenev "saw quite clearly the disadvantages of tearing myself away from my native country." But this could
not be helped. Of the environment to which he belonged,
he wrote:

That particular phase and layer of it, the serf-owning
country gentry, held nothing that could attract me.
On the contrary, nearly everything I saw around me
was embarrassing, irritating, even repugnant. I could
not hesitate any longer . . . At the risk of losing
much that was dear to me . . . I plunged headlong into
the "German-Sea" which I expected to purify and
to regenerate me. When I finally emerged from its
waves I nevertheless found myself to be a Westerner,
and a Westerner I have remained . . . There was no
other way for me . . . I could not breathe the same
air, could not remain in close contact with the thing
I hated; probably I lacked the necessary self-control
and strength of character. I had to get away from
my enemy in order to attack him the more vigorously

from a distance. That enemy had a definite shape
in my eyes, he bore a well-known name: the enemy
was serfdom. This name covered all that which I
resolved to fight against to the bitter end, all that
with which I swore never to compromise. This was
my Hannibal's oath, and I was not alone in taking it.
It was the better to keep this oath that I went to the
West. I do not think that my Westernism has
deprived me of my sympathy with Russian life, of
my understanding of its peculiarities and needs.
The Huntsman Diary, then a new venture, was
written abroad, some of the sketches at a time when
I was deeply concerned with the question whether
or not I ought to return . . . I must add that I have
never admitted the impassable line which some
zealous but uninformed patriots wish to draw
between Russia and Western Europe.

Turgenev's writings prior to his mother's death in 1853,
and his introduction to the 1880 Moscow edition of his
works help us to understand how wide was the gulf which
divided him from his mother's world and what it meant in
those days for mother and son to disagree on moral issues.
The distance between their two worlds was the distance
between two ages—between mediævalism and modernity,
between feudalism and the humanitarian ideal, the modern
trend being understood by Turgenev not in the sense of
capitalist competition but of the movement towards freedom and individualism. (In 1851 Herzen was to face the
problem of " dehumanised capitalism," later ascribed in
Russia to the failure of Liberalism, and to help to inaugur-
ate the Peasant Myth, " Populism," as a means for Russia
to avoid the brutality and efficient intolerance of the era
of capitalism.)

By the time of Mme. Turgenev's vagaries, a movement

of humanitarian, rather than political or social, opposition
to serfdom had gained firm ground in Russia; it included
the sovereign himself, for Nicholas I, no less than his elder
brother, was enough of a European to regard serfdom as a
disgrace. But the distance between the diffusion of an
idea and its application in practice may be great. The
Latin world took many centuries to prepare itself for the
abolition of slavery. The humanitarian movement of
Voltaire and of Rousseau originated in a society in which
serfdom still existed, and the two co-existed in Russia for
nearly a hundred years. That so much time should have
passed before thought was turned into action was excused
by some foreign observers of Russian serfdom, but never
by those Russians who were involved in the ferment of
ideas which, from the forties onwards, subjected the whole
social structure to a critical analysis. Those of them who
felt powerless to affect the issue nevertheless suffered in
their conscience. Turgenev too seems to have felt guilty
of a certain passivity when, at the age of twenty-six he
wrote in *Andrey Kolosov* this cryptic sentence: " Which
of us is capable of resisting the mean vanity of shallow
good feelings of charity and remorse? " The " shallow-
ness and meanness " of these feelings suggests that they
were too weak to inspire resolute action. Prince Mirsky
castigates Turgenev for what he calls " effeminate,
romantic and passive pessimism," which, he argues, is not
characteristic of Russia but of the cosmopolitan Europe
of the nineteenth century. (*Modern Russian Literature*,
p. 32).

Turgenev could neither despise nor hate his mother,
who appears as a fine specimen of Bergson's Creative
Evolution, passionate and irrational, and who shared—
though only up to a point—the modern totalitarian's
belief in her day to day conduct that it was the only kind

that worked. Her pragmatism was far from complete; at times she was overcome by what distinguishes the Christian, however imperfect, from the totalitarian and the pragmatist: an overwhelming sense of sin.

Could Mme. Turgenev claim, as despots and their sycophants do, that her system worked? That the people round her, if only they would obey blindly, would have no reason to be unhappy? Within the restricted limits of material needs, it must be admitted that her household and the several thousand serfs whom she probably owned, especially those who lived at a distance from her, had tolerable conditions and were, perhaps, better off than during the subsequent period of Liberty.

Progress in Russia has always been patchy. Turgenev's " enemy " was not a homogenous phenomenon common to the whole of Russia. Turgenev, in his introduction to *From a Sportsman's Notes* (1847) describes the contrast between peasant life in the Province of Orel and in the Province of Kaluga, only sixty miles away. The Kostroma serfs, described in *Khor and Kalinich*, were relatively freer, because in their area a yearly rent (*obrok*), payable to the masters, left them at liberty to earn their living in their own way. In other places they were bound to personal services on the Home Farm or the lands reserved by the master, an additional burden which was legally limited but depended in fact on the demands of the agent or of the owner.

Where the owner resided on the estate a greater proportion of the serfs was absorbed into his household and experienced the advantages and the disadvantages of closer contact with his family and his senior subordinates. Domestic serfs play a large part in Madame Turgenev's household. They fulfil a variety of functions, ranging from menial work to professional services, and combine their state of subjection to a tyrannical power with loyal devotion and even intimacy. In the small household of Dostoevsky's father, one of them, driven to despair, killed his master.

Law was on the side of the owners, and A. F. Koni (born in 1844), a prominent judge, forensic orator and writer, has thrown an interesting light on the peasant "revolts" frequently mentioned between 1828 and 1851. The growing danger of peasant discontent caused a law to be enacted, and stiffened in the forties, authorising the owners to have objectionable serfs deported to Siberia together with their families. Little was needed to substantiate the request, which had to be sent to the provincial authorities with the costs of transportation as far as Irkutsk. Here the deportee, after travelling in one of the weekly or monthly convoys of criminals, was turned into a settler. Koni believes that many of the complaints lodged by the owners (particularly by the women) and referring to "revolts," arose merely out of cases of recalcitrance, ill will, spite, jealousy or the many other petty causes of bitterness among members of a household. This would explain Mme. Turgenev's threats against her serfs, threats which were not, however, carried into effect.

Along with serfdom, Turgenev in his early writings describes the poor squires in the households of the better off (cf. translation by M. S. Mansell, Heinemann, 1942). Even the servants took liberties with these toadies. *The Family Charge* (1848) dramatically presents such a humble Lazarus, and his revolt. Fourteen years later Turgenev published *Fathers and Sons*, conceived during his stay in the Isle of Wight and written in Paris and in Russia. By this time the intellectual proletariat had entered the scene of Russian history, its ranks swelled by the ever-growing number of impoverished squires

Turgenev, contrary to what contemporary critics thought, was attracted by their straight-forward pugnacity. Sketched on the eve of the abolition of serfdom his portrait of the intellectual " of no importance " is, well and truly, a farewell to the era of serfdom and of the refinement of wealth.

At the same date Pisarev, a youngster " of good family,' aged twenty-one and serving his first year of imprisonment in the Fortress of Sts. Peter and Paul, but allowed to go on publishing his monthly reviews (*pace* Stalin), sounded the knell of the old order. His ideas became the stock in trade of the younger generation, and of H. G. Wells, born four years later. It took some time for the young Russian intellectuals eagerly absorbing the repetitive and redundant fluency of Pisarev's style to conform to the new pattern, of which Turgenev actually met an early specimen (the country doctor in *Fathers and Sons*) in whom he recognised the coming type.

Turgenev should thus have seemed to be in league with the future, but he was not accepted as such, chiefly because of the hundred little mannerisms which he fastened on to the " New Man," making the description to appear as a satire, just as, on his own admission, he almost caricatured the older generation and its conventions. Another political suspect, Chernyshevsky, had already chosen a model revolutionary for the hero of his novel *What is to be Done?* But this was not Turgenev's way. He merely recorded life as he saw it at the time of his great novels; and he saw it " moving," not stationary as in his earlier period, when his mother was still alive, and when the existing order was already criticised but the characteristics of the " New Man " could only be imagined.

A character such as his mother's was immovable. She had taken up her posture in life. The only force which might perhaps have altered her was, it seems, her beloved son. He tried several times, but she always out-manœuvered him. (I suspect that something similar happened to him with Mme. Viardot, the great French singer, the idol of his life.)

It is interesting to compare the young Turgenev, as he appears in the memoirs, with the portraits of him drawn by his contemporaries at a later date. There are several references to him in the correspondence of that shrewd observer, Countess A. A. Tolstoy, Leo Tolstoy's clever aunt. She accuses Turgenev of "superficiality" and "heartlessness." Asked by her why there are never any children in his novels, he appears struck by the remark which nobody had made to him before, and, to her question whether he is fond of children he answers frankly: "No, I don't like children." There follow observations on his religious indifference, his disbelief in immortality, his off-hand references to the Gospels, and the writer concludes that his contrast with Tolstoy is complete: no depth, a house built on sand. Such was Turgenev ten or fifteen years after his mother's death, or so he appeared in conversation with Countess Tolstoy, at that time governess to the future Duchess of Edinburgh.

Yet it is not hard to believe that the very different portrait drawn by Zhitova is equally life-like. The explanation seems to me simple. The intransigent political moralists among Russian literary critics have no patience with the change wrought by age and experience in the moral and political passions of youth. Yet few are more exposed to the fading of such passions than the man revealed by Turgenev's plays, especially the plays written in his mother's lifetime. The method he adopts, and in which he excels, of portraying his characters is an intense concentration on their manners. Elusive elements of vulgarity which would be overlooked by less sensitive and observant natures are, to him, glaring and omnipresent. The young Turgenev seems indeed to be incapable of inattention to manners; and such he appears even in later life, when, to judge from the few specimens in the Soviet catalogue of his correspondence, his letters to his daughter insist, above all, on the correct French wording of her letters to him. Æsthetic sensitiveness may induce æsthetic indignation, but it is apt to blunt the capacity for moral indignation. Nothing is further removed from Turgenev's nature than the revolutionary Promethean spirit. In describing this spirit with understanding he still remains alive to the danger of self-righteous vanity.

He was the last person whom moral indignation, however adequate its grounds, would have forced into a family quarrel, above all a quarrel with his mother. In one Russian novel after another, almost to the point of becoming a *cliché*, conflicts between young and old break out for much slighter reasons than those which emerged in Turgenev's talk with his mother about the three things which she could not admit: the iniquity of serfdom, the clandestine marriage of her eldest son and her younger son's choice of a career as a writer. The grounds of disagreement were sufficiently wide, yet Ivan continued to behave as a respectful son. Many Russian readers, perhaps the majority, have condemned him for this. Yet perhaps in England his filial restraint would be more easily excused. For have we not here a striking example of tolerance coupled with good manners, an example so intolerable to the Russian intelligentsia, but less repugnant to the older civilisation.

Turgenev, we feel, was also actuated by something deeper than good manners or the " constructive understanding " of the pedagogue or the politician waiting for the curative effects of time. (Understanding proved, indeed, singularly unconstructive. Mme. Turgenev was of an unusual " toughness.") His mother, as she appears in the memoirs, could not be a happy woman. Her strong will and her lust for power must have given her moments of satisfaction but never of joy; and of her two sons only one could have given her this. How could Turgenev fail to have compassion: his mother's was surely the most needy soul that he was ever to meet.

To borrow G. M. Trevelyan's adjectives, she was self-poised, self-judged, but not self-approved.

*   *   *   *

While assisting Miss Mills in her arduous task I have often admired her patience in seeking out the exact English equivalent of the many colloquialisms used so aptly in the original text. Perhaps the reader will understand her enthusiasm, as well as my own persistence in seeing the thing through, despite the difficulties of working at a distance from libraries, where even the Russian text would have been unavailable had it not been for the loan of a copy from the School of Slavonic Studies and the kindness of its Librarian, Dr. Loewenson.

A. MEYENDORFF.

Chapter One

EARLY LIFE OF BARBARA PETROVNA

A FEW days after my birth in the year 1833, I was taken to the house of Barbara Petrovna Turgenev, mother of the writer, Ivan Sergeyevitch Turgenev. By her wish, and with the consent of my parents, I was to be educated by her, or rather to be brought up as her adopted daughter. As will be seen in my reminiscences of the Turgenev Family, I remained with Barbara Petrovna till the day of her death, which took place on the 16th of November, 1850, in Moscow, at Ostozhenka, in the Lochakovsky house, opposite the commercial school.

There were two of us at her death bed: Nicholas Sergeyevich, her elder son, and I.

Ivan Sergeyevich was at that time in Petersburg. The late Theodore Ivanovich Inozemtsev[1] had previously foretold almost the exact date of Barbara Petrovna's death; why Ivan did not arrive sooner, or whether he had been informed in good time of his mother's approaching end, I do not know.

He arrived in Moscow in the evening, on the day of the funeral, when we had already returned from the cemetery of the Donskoy monastery, where Barbara Petrovna was buried.[2]

In the course of seventeen years, which I spent almost uninterruptedly with her, I saw and heard much that was so closely connected with our general favourite, Turgenev, that I hope it will not be without interest to his admirers.

---

[1] A famous medical man born 1802, died 1869.
[2] *The Mongols* by Dmitry Donskoy (near the Don) in 1380.

Fortunately, I have kept the letters that Barbara Petrovna wrote to me during our rare separations, her sons' letters to me, and the letters of close family connections.

All this correspondence, and the album with its remarks and advice to her sons (all in Barbara Petrovna's own hand) have been a very great help to me in arranging these memoirs, and have very much refreshed my memory. I cannot, of course, observe a complete chronological order ; I must go backwards and forwards, but that does not interfere with the accuracy and truth of the story.

In a few fragmentary tales about Barbara Petrovna in newspapers and magazines of the current year (1884) that have come into my possession, I have read anecdotes about her that were not always just, and which represented her in anything but a sympathetic light ; in truth, she may probably appear in such a light in my stories ; but, as I was formerly very near to her, as I enjoyed her love and had myself a boundless love for her, I consider it my duty to point out those circumstances in her life which had had such a prejudicial effect on so proud and passionate a nature as Barbara Petrovna's.

But—other times—other manners.

Her childhood and youth were spent in such painful, revolting circumstances that it would not have been surprising if so much unhappiness had embittered her character, and stifled in her those good impulses with which her nature was endowed.

In her veins flowed the blood of the Lutovinovs, unrestrained and at that time almost all-powerful landowners. The Lutovinov family was then well known in the district and province as a bold and violent type of squire, and it was not the only one.

In his novel *Three Portraits*, and in his tale *The*

Freeholder Ovsyannikov, Ivan Sergeyevich is really speaking about his own ancestors. Barbara Petrovna's mother, Katherine Ivanovna Lutovinov, was not distinguished for gentleness of character either, and if we acknowledge the law of heredity which considers character inborn, then Barbara Petrovna's ought to have been one of the harshest ; but we cannot call it evil, because sometimes Barbara Petrovna revealed impulses of tenderness, goodness and humanity which gave evidence of a heart far from unfeeling.

Her egoism, love of power, and sometimes malice, were the result of cruel and humiliating treatment in childhood and youth, and of bitter disappointment in old age.

Widowed when comparatively young, Barbara Petrovna's mother married as her second husband Somov, a widower with two grown-up daughters. Katherine Ivanovna never loved the daughter of her first marriage, and, under the influence of her second husband, she became a stepmother to Barbara Petrovna and a mother to her stepdaughters, Somov's children. All Barbara Petrovna's childhood was humiliating and revolting, there were even occasions of cruel treatment. I have heard several details, but my hand refuses to portray all the horrors to which she was subjected. Somov hated her, compelled her in childhood to submit to his whims and those of his daughters, beat her, humiliated her in every way, and after a plentiful indulgence in infusions of brandy and sweet peppermint wine he vented his drunken violence on Barbara Petrovna. When she had completed her sixteenth year, he began to persecute her in another way—this was after the style of Karamazov[1] (the old man). To avoid the shame of a most humiliating punishment for her refusal to consent to this disgrace, Barbara

[1] In Dostoyevsky's famous novel *The Brothers Karamazov*.

Petrovna, with the help of her devoted nurse, Natalia Vassilyevna, succeeded in escaping from her stepfather's house.

I have not heard all the details ; I know only that, on foot, half dressed, she travelled twenty miles, and found refuge in the house of her own uncle, Ivan Ivanovich Lutovinov, then squire of the village of Spasskoye.

Her uncle took her under his protection and, in spite of her mother's demands, refused to allow her to return to her stepfather's house.

Katherine Ivanovna Somov lived at Kholodov ; and there she died. In the story "Death" (*Huntsman's Notes*) which describes her last moments, the squire's wife, who herself paid the priest for her own prayer for the dying, was Ivan Sergeyevich's own grandmother.

In her uncle's house Barbara Petrovna was free from insults and cruelty. Her uncle treated her well, although he was rather severe and miserly. He, as the saying is, kept a tight hand on her, and she lived very much in seclusion at Spasskoye. For quite a long time Barbara Petrovna had to submit to his will and his whims. She was nearly thirty years old when Ivan Ivanovich Lutovinov died.

His death was sudden, and there were many strange rumours about it ; I never knew anything definite.

On the death of her uncle, being sole heir to his great estates, Barbara Petrovna breathed the air of freedom, and apparently said to herself—Now I can do what I like.

Such a strong character and such a fiery temperament as hers, emerging into full liberty after long oppression, naturally manifested themselves in those outbursts of which signs had been shown. Hitherto, for her there had been no tenderness, no love and no freedom. Now she had absolute power in her own hands, and could do anything she liked.

From Barbara Petrovna herself I did not hear any tales about her life in her stepfather's house; but the bitter memory of what she suffered then sometimes burst out in her conversation.

"*You do not know,*" she often said to me, "*what it means to be an orphan; you are an orphan, but you have a mother in me, you are so surrounded by my love and care, that you do not feel your orphanhood.*" Or: "*To be an orphan without father and mother is hard; but to be an orphan in the sight of your own mother is horrible; that is what I suffered, my mother hated me.*"

Here is what I found in one of her letters to me. The original is dated December 15th, 1848:

"*Orphans are not children long; I was an orphan myself, and I felt my position very much in the presence of others; I was more of an orphan than you, because you have a mother, but I had not; my mother was like a stepmother; she married again; had other children, other ties, I was alone in the world.*"

On the death of her uncle, being then on the wrong side of thirty, Barbara Petrovna married Sergius Nikolaye-vich Turgenev. About him I have heard that he was angelically good, but Barbara Petrovna herself spoke only of his good looks.

At one time, and somewhere abroad, Sergius Nikolaye-vich Turgenev was presented to one of the ruling German princesses. Several years afterwards Barbara Petrovna was drinking the waters at Karlsbad; and there, at that time, was that same princess. At the fountain they happened to stand not far from each other, and when Barbara Petrovna held out her jug, there was a bracelet on her arm containing a portrait of her husband, and the princess took her by the hand with the words: " You are Turgenev's wife, I remember him; with the exception of the Emperor Alexander I, I have never seen a handsomer man than your husband."

After her marriage, Barbara Petrovna lived that full seignorial life, lived in former times by our landowners. Her wealth, her husband's good looks, her own wit and knowledge of the world, attracted to their house all who were well known and distinguished in the province of Orel. Her orchestra, singers, the theatre with its actors (who were serfs), everything in age-old Spasskoye was so attractive that everyone sought the honour of being a guest there.

Being clever and agreeable—more than that, I may say, fascinating—Barbara Petrovna, who was neither handsome nor young, and whose face was slightly pitted by smallpox, had always a crowd of admirers near her.

After long suffering and prolonged servitude, the knowledge of her own strength developed in Barbara Petrovna, that egoism and thirst for power that caused so much suffering to many of those about her.

Yet she never took such harsh and cruel advantage of her seignorial rights as did many others.

Her power, pressing heavily on all those who surrounded her, made itself grievously felt, yet she was liked; it may be that her friendly look, her cordial words, made all those people happy whose lot it was to experience them.

In her there was a mixture of kindliness, and a continual desire to bend everyone to her will; and bitterly did those suffer who were not absolutely obedient.

I have kept all her letters, filled with the warmest expressions of love and care for me; the most tender mother could not have shown greater love for her own daughter ; yet with all this she tyrannized over me, as she did over all those who were near her. In spite of this, I loved her passionately, and when I was, though rarely, separated from her, I felt lonely and unhappy.

Indeed those who loved her, and were most devoted to her, suffered most of all.

One might think that she wanted to avenge on others her own unhappy childhood and frustrated youth, and make others suffer what she herself had suffered.

What torture all this was to Ivan Sergeyevich ! And the thing that tormented him the most, was the knowledge that he could do nothing to alter it, and that any interference or intercession would only make things worse.

Chapter Two

OTHER MEMBERS OF THE TURGENEV FAMILY

My memories of the Turgenev family begin with the year 1838—the year of Ivan Sergeyevich's departure for Berlin ; several events of that time were particularly imprinted on my childish memory.

We were then living in Petersburg, in Linev's house. Ivan Sergeyevich had finished his university course, and Nicholas Sergeyevich was already an officer in the Horse Guards Artillery.

The Turgenev family, in addition to Barbara Petrovna, consisted of her brother-in-law, Nicholas Nikolayevich Turgenev, who, on the death of her husband, Sergius Nikolayevich, administered all her estates until the year 1846 ; her two sons, Nicholas and Ivan Sergeyevich, myself as " adopted daughter, the child of the house," and also a niece " three times removed " of Barbara Petrovna, Mavra Timofeyevna Slivitskaya, who was married to Artukhov, professor at the university of Kharkov. In the house there was often a succession of governesses from abroad, teachers and music mistresses for me.

In my time there were no toadeaters at Barbara Petrovna's. She was not one of those landowners who were pleased by the servility of those indebted to her for a living. Her love of power and insistence on obedience were not confined simply to her own family and to her serfs ; she ruled over all who surrounded her, or had any kind of connection with her, and withal, she revealed in herself that rare and often misunderstood moral strength that conquered even people not bound to obey her. Sometimes a look or an interjection would be enough to break off any talk to which she did not want to listen. In her presence no-one dared to express an opinion contrary to hers. Ivan Sergeyevich alone, her favourite, spoke plainly about his wishes and sympathies, but in the most gentle and considerate manner, more as if entreating than blaming.

The yoke of serfdom, specially heavy in his mother's house, made a painful impression on the mind of Ivan Sergeyevich, who was himself noted for his kindness, and what made it all the more painful was that he could not fight against it. Sometimes, however, even without a struggle, his kindliness subdued even Barbara Petrovna's will. With him she was quite different, and therefore in his presence everything felt easier. His rare visits were a blessing. When he was there, his mother not only did not imagine faults, but she even treated real faults more indulgently. She behaved as kindheartedly as if it gladdened her to see the expression of pleasure on her son's face. And what a gentle and loving son he was to his mother when I first begin to remember him!

His feeling towards his mother changed later, as I myself witnessed. The causes of such a change will be revealed by subsequent events. At the beginning of 1838 or the end of 1837 when Barbara Petrovna underwent a very serious operation, I heard, from eye-witnesses, with what tender care he surrounded his mother, and how he sat throughout the night by her bed.

During the year 1838 we led a very solitary life, owing to Barbara Petrovna's ailing condition. Daily visitors were Arendt and Gromov, well-known doctors at that time ; very often Rodion Yegorovich Grünwald, a former comrade of the late Turgenev *père* visited us, and Vassily Andreyevich Zhukovsky, whom I did not like at all then, because, nearly every time he came, I had to learn by heart some of the verses from his *Undine* and recite them to him. Though he always brought me wonderful sweets, I nevertheless showed the blackest ingratitude, because while I was sucking them my five-year-old mind considered that I should soon have in return to learn a few verses from *Undine* which Barbara Petrovna would repeat to me.

At that time I was very great friends with Ivan Sergeyevich. He was very fond of me, played with me, ran about the immense hall carrying me in his arms, and he was still so young himself, that he was not above running about and playing the schoolboy, not simply for my amusement, but for his own pleasure ; one of his schoolboy tricks I remember vividly.

For some reason or other he was very keen on the Greek language. Every afternoon someone came to him, and to my great distress I was excluded from his room during those hours ; I listened behind the door to some kind of incomprehensible sounds, pronounced now in Ivan Sergeyevich's voice, now in that of his teacher or comrade. But I happened to take part in the study of Aristophanes. Once he took it into his head to teach me " frog Greek " as he called it. My knowledge was confined to this, that he made me learn the following sounds " Bre-ke-ke-keks-koaks-koaks ! "[1]

Having received this quasi-Greek information, I was stood on the table, given some sort of allegedly classical pose, with one hand stretched out, and made to repeat what I had learned, at first slowly, almost solemnly, but afterwards very quickly, and in the shrillest, most squeaky voice ; at this, we both burst into such an immense fit

[1] Thanks to a classicist of my acquaintance, I am convinced that my memory has not betrayed me. The sounds, with which Ivan Sergeyevich amused us so much, are reproduced in the comedy of Aristophanes, *The Frogs*.

of laughter that our performance attracted Barbara
Petrovna's attention to us, and she then came out to
check us :

"*Finissez donc, Jean, vous gâtez la petite, vous en ferez
une virago!*" Sometimes in our noisiest moments of
enthusiasm at our performance, mamma's maid would
come to quieten us. She came in with noiseless tread,
and in a severe and imposing manner said: "Mamma
orders you to stop." We were silent, and to comfort me,
Ivan Sergeyevich seated me on his shoulder, and
triumphantly carried me round the room.

All this happened when Ivan Sergeyevich was quite
young ; then he still laughed with the careless, rolling
infectious laughter of a happy man, and his laughter was
sometimes so loud, that his mother very seriously and
severely checked him. "*Mais cessez donc, Jean, c'est
mauvais genre de rire ainsi.*" Qu'est-ce que ce rire
bourgeois!*"

Often afterwards Barbara Petrovna remembered his
" bourgeois laugh "; but on his return from Berlin we
never again heard that laugh. He was considered to be
a very cheerful talker, really jolly, but he was very rarely
so at home.

I remember very distinctly the day when Ivan
Sergeyevich went abroad. In the morning we all went
to the Kazan Cathedral, where we took part in the service of prayer for travellers. Barbara Petrovna sat the
whole time on a folding chair and wept bitterly. She,
Nicholas and I accompanied him to the steamer.

On our return from the docks, when Barbara Petrovna
was seated in the carriage, she fainted.

A few days afterwards we went to Spasskoye. There,
we received letters from Ivan Sergeyevich offering a
thanksgiving for his deliverance from the fire on board

ship, and later, a water colour portrait was sent from Berlin.[1]

It was a striking likeness, and I remember now my cry of childish ecstasy: *C'est Jean* when I was shown the portrait. Barbara Petrovna never parted with it, it always stood on her writing table, and, when she went into the country, or to Moscow in the winter, she always packed it herself in her travelling bag.

The separation from her son caused her much suffering. I have kept her album dated 1839 and 1840. I quote from it a few lines, expressive of her love for her son, and her longing for him.

" 1839. *A mon fils, Jean.*

" *C'est que Jean est mon soleil à moi ; je ne vois que lui, et lorsqu'il s'eclipse, je ne vois plus clair, je ne sais plus où j'en suis. Le coeur d'une mère ne se trompe jamais, et Vous savez Jean, que mon instinct est plus sûr que ma raison.*"

I read somewhere that Barbara Petrovna left her diary to her son.

In the summer of 1849, at Spasskoye, in the flower garden opposite that Casino (the name of which eventually became famous because of its association with Ivan Sergeyevich), Barbara Petrovna's diaries and correspondence were burnt, by her order and in her presence, and I personally assisted at this *auto-da-fé*.

In 1849 and 1850 she continued to write her diary in pencil and on separate sheets of paper. A few days after her death Nicholas Sergeyevich took these papers into his mother's study, closed the door, and read them aloud ; his wife, Ivan Sergeyevich and I were his hearers.

Where these papers are now, I do not know ; I remember their contents, but I do not think that Ivan Sergeyevich would ever have wished to make them public.

[1] A copy of this portrait appeared in the *European Messenger*, 1884, but the original is in the possession of the author of the memoirs.—ED.

Chapter Three

THE FIRE AT SPASSKOYE

In some families there are events which always remain in their memory, and in the memory of those connected with them. Such an event was the fire in the great house at Spasskoye. It was a landmark in the Turgenev family, and therefore it was generally said: Such and such a thing happened before the fire, or after the fire.

The fire was on the 3rd of May, 1839.

Nicholas Sergeyevich, Barbara Petrovna's elder son, who was serving in the army, was that year appointed officer in charge of the remount. On his way to Lebedyan[1] he stayed for a few days with his mother, on the night of the fire he was due to leave.

On account of Nicholas Sergeyevich's departure, supper was ordered to be served earlier than usual.

At nine o'clock, the old butler, Anton Gregoryevich,[2] who a few minutes before had set the table, came in with a basket and quickly began to put in it all the silver from the table—forks, knives and spoons.

"What are you doing, Anton?" asked Barbara Petrovna. "Are you drunk?"

"Not at all, madame, but we can't have any supper."

"Why not? . . ." But Barbara Petrovna's cry was accompanied by an unusual light, that lit up all the room.

"What is it—lightning?"

Just then Nicholas Sergeyevich ran in.

"Mamma, take your money, jewels, anything valuable; we are on fire."

---

[1] A district town in the province of Tambov.
[2] Known in Mumu by the name of Uncle Khvost, a man of singular cowardice.

"Where is the fire?"—Barbara Petrovna still did not understand.

"Yes, yes, quickly, mamma"...Nicholas Sergeyevich urged her on; I rushed to Vassilyevna; he ran out of the room.

It seems that the fire broke out first in the left wing of the house, where lived a very old and helpless woman, Barbara Petrovna's nurse, Natalia Vassilyevna, the same who had helped her to escape from her stepfather's house.

In the confusion caused by the fire, everyone except Nicholas Sergeyevich had forgotten the poor old woman: he remembered her, and hastened to her assistance.

This is what we saw, when Barbara Petrovna, holding me by the hand, came out of the burning building; the whole wing was on fire, and on the stairs was Nicholas Sergeyevich, carrying the unfortunate Natalia Vassilyevna.

"My angel, my deliverer!" she cried, "leave me! You will be burned yourself, leave me, master!"

But Nicholas Sergeyevich's exploit ended happily; he succeeded in rescuing the unfortunate woman from the flames.

The old woman lived for some years after that, and her favourite topic of conversation was always the story of how her "angel master, with his own hands had saved her, a useless old woman, from the fire, and prevented her dying a terrible death, without time for repentance."

When we came out of the house, Barbara Petrovna sat in an armchair near the porch, and everything that was brought out of the house was put near her.

Many willingly helped to save the family possessions; but many also did not forget themselves; for instance, one of the peasants was on the point of walking off with the twenty thousand roubles entrusted to Nicholas Sergeyevich by the Crown for buying horses.

The year 1839 was memorable in the Turgenev family not only for the fire, but for another reason as well. That year saw the beginning of Nicholas Sergeyevich's love for Anna Yakovlevna Schwartz (afterwards his wife), and in consequence of that same fire, they were brought closer together: Nicholas Sergeyevich saved his mother's old nurse from the flames, and Anna Yakovlevna courageously snatched the box containing the twenty thousand roubles out of the hands of the peasant who was running off with it.

Taking advantage of the confusion, the thief had managed to get some distance beyond the iron fence enclosing the Spasskoye grounds. Anna Yakovlevna overtook him, took the box from him, and with this heavy burden went back to where Barbara Petrovna was sitting, and there almost fainted.

Much of the Lutovinov property was destroyed that day. Nearly all the family portraits were burnt ; much was looted ; the outer staircase of the store-room, containing the most valuable services of Chinese and Sèvres porcelain, and all the silver was forgotten, and therefore very little was saved.

Afterwards, on clearing up the site of the fire, several bars of blackened silver were found. These bars had assumed the most extraordinary shapes, and were then placed, as a kind of decoration, on Barbara Petrovna's writing table.

The house burned for a long time, and for a long time we sat near the porch ; when the roof at last fell in, Nicholas Sergeyevich came to us with the phæton and a pair of horses, put his mother and me in the carriage, and drove us himself to Petrovskoye, a little village about a verst and a half from Spasskoye, Barbara Petrovna's birthplace.

Some time before, the little Petrovskoye house had been turned into an almshouse, where five or six old women were ending their lives in various ways.

And now Barbara Petrovna had to leave her rich, luxurious Spasskoye house, and settle for a time in the house given by her for the use of her poor.

In the hall of this little house, in the single unoccupied room, there was one divan only.

With tender care Barbara Petrovna put me on it, assuring me that the fire was over, and my doll, which in some way or other had been uninjured in my arms, she put near me.

The right wing only of the house was not burned, and it was soon made ready to live in; several additions were made to it, so that, joined to the uninjured stone gallery that was turned into a library, the place was made roomy enough, and the wing was even called a house.

When, on Barbara Petrovna's death, Spasskoye passed into Ivan Sergeyevich's hands, he stayed there nearly every summer, and until recently its outward appearance was not altered.

When we first went into this so-called new house, I was astonished at the simplicity of its interior decoration, and for a long time, I thought of our little drawing room in the old house, with pictures on the walls instead of paper, and the luxurious furniture covered in yellow leather. The backs of the divans and armchairs of this furniture were ebony, with ornamentation in bronze.

These decorations were of a symbolic character: a whole row of Cupids and lions; every Cupid was leading a lion on a chain interwoven with flowers. And all this was burned. The only thing that was whole was an immense mirror, and that, owing to its size, could not find a place in the new house; it was taken to Moscow, and until Barbara Petrovna's death was in the hall, where it was often a source of surprise to visitors, owing to its beauty and its size. The last time I saw this mirror was after Nicholas Sergeyevich's death, in the house of Madame Malyarevskaya, niece of Nicholas Sergeyevich's wife.

Before continuing my reminiscences of my earlier life in Barbara Petrovna's house, I wish to digress a little.

Several stories about Turgenev's mother that appeared in magazines and newspapers on the death of Ivan Sergeyevich, compel me to stop for a while, and describe Barbara Petrovna's life and character. I hope that my reminiscences will explain them more clearly, and will take away from Barbara Petrovna that appearance of almost caricatured eccentricity put upon her by these stories, stories that were drawn from unreliable sources, from people who did not live with her, and who neither knew nor understood her, stories added to and exaggerated by imagination, and which have already become legendary.

Judging by one of these stories, it would appear that from the year 1840, which I, with the exception of only a few details, thoroughly and clearly remember, Barbara Petrovna wished to appear humble (as her son suggested later in *Virgin Soil*) and at the same time quite the reverse.

But I had never noticed in her any wish to appear a person of importance.

True, she belonged to the landed gentry; she was a lover of power and a despot, and she showed herself capricious and tyrannical, but there were in her impulses of magnanimity and kindness natural to the most humane. Her bearing was one of proud dignity, she required absolute obedience to her will, but she had frequently a kind word for her favourites.

She bore every material loss with unusual calmness. The Spasskoye fire was a great loss, but neither a sigh nor a groan was heard from her. Once, when some over-loaded boats went to the bottom carrying forty thousand roubles worth of corn, she never turned a hair.

She did not call her rooms "apartments," and with the exception of an additional building called the "Casino," the rest of her rooms had the simplest names. The interior rooms were: bedroom, dressing-room and wardrobe room. Entrance into these rooms was per-mitted to her chief chambermaid and two of her assistants among the women servants, and among the men, only to Doctor Porphyry Timofeyevich (a serf) . . . and when she was ill, then the steward, the chief clerk and the cook also came "for orders."

Her sons sometimes visited her in her bedroom, but they invariably asked permission beforehand, because Barbara Petrovna was always unusually punctilious in her dress and her habits. She was never seen when she was at all untidy, and even when she was ill, would put on a smart *négligé*.

In her youth, they say she was ugly, but when old, I found her almost handsome, and always beautifully and elegantly dressed. Her caps were of rich tulle, with lavish trimming, and a coquettish bow of coloured ribbon at the side; her morning gowns were of an extraordinary yet elegant style, and sometimes they were so original that only such a *grande dame* as herself could have looked distinguished, handsome and smart in them. She had a numerous staff of personal household servants, about forty; but no-one was called by any kind of unusual name: they were butler, steward, *valet-de-chambre*, clerk, cashier, business agents, and there were errand boys, but not called pretentiously "Cossacks," and without distinguishing badge on their breast. Their duty was to be in daily attendance at her door, and to transmit their mistress's orders, or they were sent on errands.

Of the women servants, only one, her chief chambermaid, was called "maid of honour" or "lady in waiting" to her mistress; but at that time that was the usual description. The rest were: keeper of the linen, laundry maids, sewing maids, dressmakers, embroiderers, and simply maid-servants.

Her managers were German and Russian, and were called by their Christian names, except one, a Greek, who was called Zosimych. "Call Zosimych," Barbara Petrovna would say. All those servants who were about her had to be able to read and write, and one girl was even taught French with me, so that she could copy from books, because Barbara Petrovna, who read only French novels, liked to take extracts from them. It was really for this that the girl was taught to read and write French . . . and she had to copy from books the parts pointed out by Barbara Petrovna's pencil.

Twice a week the postillion Gavryushka came to bring and take away the correspondence. He came up to the house with a little bell, but not a very noisy one, and I can hear it now, every week before our provincial post goes.

With regard to those admitted to her presence, Barbara Petrovna was really very particular. For example, during all the time that I lived with her, I never saw one person belonging to the police force. They came on business . . . but only to the office, and when they were a few hundred yards away from it, they had to unfasten the bell, so that they would not disturb Barbara Petrovna. In her aristocratic house there was no place for the police. I, of course, thought that these men were like those of the times described in *Dead Souls*[1] and *Provincial Sketches*.[2]

Only our district police inspector, Shepsky, whom Barbara Petrovna very much liked, would drive up to the house itself, ringing a little bell. The district doctor, Peter Alexandrovich Sokolov, came with his little bell to the wing, because he was considered to be a shade lower than the police inspector, and he entered the house from the wing. Strict order was maintained in Barbara Petrovna's house and mode of living, everything was done to time. Even the doves that she fed at Spasskoye and in Moscow knew their time; at twelve noon a bell rang, and they flew to take their portion of oats.

Barbara Petrovna was very fond of birds, but not specially of hens and poultry . . . these feathered creatures had their poultry yard far enough away from the house, so that their clucking and clacking would not disturb her. The birds, canaries, greenfinches, goldfinches, and the " inseparable " parrots, were kept in the house in dainty cages.

[1] by Gogol.
[2] by Shchedrin.

Chapter Four

FAITHFUL SERVANTS

BARBARA PETROVNA spoke Russian only to the servants, and generally we all at that time read, wrote, spoke, thought and even prayed in French. I had already learnt the Russian prayers and Philaret's[1] catechism when I went to the boarding school kept by Madame Knol, and was studying for an examination. I was then fourteen years old.

This is how I began the morning; my eyes were scarcely open when I had to repeat aloud the following prayer: *"Seigneur, donnez-moi la force pour résister, la patience pour souffrir, et la constance pour persévérer."*

These words, then repeated thoughtlessly and mechanically, were prophetic. I have had much need of strength, patience and the will to persevere.

In addition, I had to read aloud every morning a chapter from the *Imitation of Jesus Christ* by Thomas à Kempis, and when I was separated from Barbara Petrovna she constantly ordered me in her letters to read this book every day.

We used the French language and prayers so much that, when we prepared for Communion, after the reading of the rules by the priest at home, I even said the prayer before Holy Communion in French.

Soon after the fire, that is at the end of June, Barbara Petrovna and I went on a pilgrimage to Voronezh. On the way there, at the inn at Elyets,[2] I caught smallpox, prevalent at that time, and because of this we stayed for

---

[1] 1782-1867. Metropolitan of Moscow from 1826.
[2] In the province of Orel.

about three months at Voronezh, until I had quite recovered. Probably every doctor in Voronezh was sent for to treat me ; but I owe my life, and the fact that this terrible disease left no trace, to the care of Barbara Petrovna's chief chambermaid, Agatha.

In the day-time, Barbara Petrovna herself, Anna Yakov-levna Schwartz, and others, were continually present at my bedside, but at night Agatha, then little more than twenty years old, did not sleep for a moment, so that I should not even touch my face.

And that was not the least of Agatha's services for me. If I were writing my own life, I would say a great deal about her, my dear old friend ; I would tell all that she was for me ; how she, by her example as a wife, and her self-sacrifice as a mother, had a beneficial influence on my whole life. I would say much about those sacrifices that she made for me, a lonely orphan, when, on the death of Barbara Petrovna, I was left alone in the world. If not she, then may her children read these lines, and love her still more for those sorrows that she endured for them, and because in her heart which was filled with love for them, she still found a place for me, who cherish for her the warmest feelings of love and gratitude.

Agatha and her husband were Barbara Petrovna's most devoted servants, and at the same time, the chief sufferers from her despotism.

But both her sons loved and esteemed Agatha and her husband, especially Ivan Sergeyevich ; to the end of his life he kept up a correspondence with them, and when he came to Moscow after the death of his mother, he always sent for them, gave them generous presents, and asked to have all their children brought to him. The whole family was entirely worthy of Ivan Sergeyevich's consideration, and in his intercourse with them, he was always most anxious to try and make them forget the sufferings they had endured in his mother's house.

Agatha Semyonovna is still living, but her husband died in 1879. Agatha Simonovna, as everyone called her, was for nineteen years Barbara Petrovna's principal maid. At that time, all rich landowners had a servants' aristocracy, most closely attached to its masters from generation to generation. There was this aristocracy among the servants in the Turgenev house, and at its head were Agatha and her husband, Andrew Ivanovich Polyakov,[1] as secretary and chief steward. Polyakov and several others, among them Porphyry Timofeyevich, Barbara Petrovna's doctor (a serf, who was the tutor who accompanied Ivan Sergeyevich to Berlin), were all brought up with their young masters, Nicholas and Ivan. They were not sent out of the schoolroom at lesson time, so that they could do more than read and write . . . they were almost well educated.

Porphyry Timofeyevich spoke German excellently, and Polyakov spoke and wrote French, knew Russian to perfection, and sometimes even wrote verses. He was my first Russian teacher, from him I learned to read and write and the first four rules of arithmetic, and during our lessons, given in the presence of my French governess, Mdlle. Tourniard, he very fluently conversed with her in French.

All the important papers relating to the estates, all the Turgenev notes and ready cash, were in Andrew's charge.

In Agatha's hands were the rest of Barbara Petrovna's possessions. Linen, silver, lace, whole boxes full of needlework on lawn and canvas ; fruits of the labours of the so-called lace makers and embroiderers, who, in

---

[1] By the wish of their children I have given them fictitious names in my reminiscences.

winter, spun skeins of incredible fineness, and in summer, embroidered and made lace; all jewels, pearls, articles of gold, boxes of shawls, handkerchiefs, silk material, etc., were all in the care of the most reliable Agatha Simonovna, and were set apart for my trousseau.

They had occupied these positions for several years, when in 1842, Barbara Petrovna suddenly took it into her head to arrange a marriage between these, her two principal and most faithful servants. Whether this marriage would be agreeable to them, or whether they liked each other, Barbara Petrovna never troubled to ask . . . she wished it, which, being translated, means she ordered it, therefore it was so.

This marriage, however, did not take place quite like others. Agatha was a privileged being; the money for her trousseau was given by Barbara Petrovna herself, and it was made in the house, in the maids' room. In honour of the bride and bridegroom an evening party was held in a side building, and attended by the girls and young menservants. They sang songs, danced, regaled themselves with gingerbread, confectionery and nuts, all at their mistress's expense, and she herself often came to look at the gay scene.

The party the evening before the wedding was splendidly celebrated; all ceremonies and customs were observed, even to the presenting by the bridegroom to the bride of a marriage basket with ribbons, scents, pomades, and everything that belonged to such a present, and Barbara Petrovna's generosity paid for all.

At the ceremony, Barbara Petrovna herself presented her with an icon in a silver frame, taken from the icon case of the Lutovinov family. As well as the trousseau the bride received five-hundred roubles in notes. The marriage took place in the morning, and in the hall

of the manor house, a table adorned with flowers was
arranged for a banquet.   The health of the young couple
was drunk in real champagne, and Barbara Petrovna herself proposed the first toast.   All this generosity and all
this splendour were the prelude to long years of misery
and woe!

This marriage, unexpected and by order, turned out,
however, to be very happy.   Both were intelligent, good
and honest, and probably these good qualities contributed
to a complete agreement between them, and brought an
enviable happiness into their married life.

When Agatha's first daughter was born, Barbara
Petrovna was very considerate of the mother's health;
she gave her time to recover and did not hasten her
return to her duties, but, as soon as the young mother
appeared before her mistress, she was met by an
unexpected disappointment.

" How glad I am to have you with me again . . . . " were
Barbara Petrovna's first words, " . . . nothing is right without you, no-one pleases me, and I am quite dissatisfied.
But now, find some woman in the village to be a nurse
for your little one, and I will send her to Petrovsky.   I
cannot have a child here ; how could you look after me ?
You would always be going to her, you would have to
feed her, and I should have to look after myself."

The poor mother was petrified at these words, but she
dared not object.   And who did dare to object?   There
was no appeal against Barbara Petrovna's decrees.

Arrangements were made to send the child to a nurse
in the neighbouring village . . . but not carried out.

Fortunately, and very much to their credit, among all
Barbara Petrovna's numerous servants, there was not one
tell-tale.   Much was done that was not according to her
orders, much was hidden from her, and not once did

anyone report to her anything that would rouse her anger.

So it was this time; Agatha Semyonovna's child was not sent to the village, and the mother who had to be with her mistress day and night, nursed her little one herself, on the quiet. In the daytime, it was carried by a roundabout way through the garden into the wing, and at night it was in a side building separated from the house by a large entrance hall, so that even when the doors and windows were open, Barbara Petrovna could not hear the child's cry. My esteemed governess, Miss Blackwood, occupied a room in this building, and she often got up in the night to soothe the cries, or quietly, almost noiselessly to open the door, and call the mother, who slept in a room beyond her mistress's bedroom.

I was once the cause of what was nearly a great misfortune. Mamma was not well and had dined later than usual in her bedroom. Agatha was waiting on her, and I, knowing that the little one was in my governess's room, went off to look at her. There was no-one in the room, and in the basket the baby was screaming frantically for her mother. I was foolish enough to imagine that if I took her out on the porch, she would be quiet. It was in the summer, and I at once caught her up in my arms, and went out; for a moment indeed, the little one was quiet, then, feeling that she had been deceived, she cried louder than ever. The door was open, Barbara Petrovna heard the cry.

"What is that?" . . . and she said this in such an angry voice, and with such a piercing look at Agatha, that the poor woman became pale as death, too confused to know what to say. The father, however, darted wildly out of the house, tore the child from my arms, and, pressing his hand pitilessly over her mouth, rushed headlong through the garden into the wing, and I, recognising the thoughtlessness of my action, was so terrified and in such despair, that even now, I do not understand how the storm passed by. I know only that, for a long time after this, Barbara Petrovna regarded the father and mother very suspiciously and severely, and every day she went into the wing.

And it was in this way, always in fear and trembling, on the stairs, and in the rain or cold, that poor Agatha had to nurse her three children. Barbara Petrovna provided a nannie for the older ones, but again and again she ordered the youngest to be sent to be nursed by some peasant. Left to strangers, the unfortunate little ones were sometimes sick, and the poor mother could only see them about twice a day, when she was free to dine, sup or have tea. And vividly do I now see her beautiful, expressive eyes, fixed either in entreaty or reproach on the icons !

"Why, why ? " it seemed as if she wanted to say through her tightly-shut lips.

One of the most terrible dramas in her much afflicted life took place after the birth of her third daughter.

In the December of that year, Barbara Petrovna left Spasskoye for Moscow. Agatha Semyonovna was to follow her in a week or two, and she was given strict orders to settle the children at Spasskoye, and not bring any of them with her. But the tender heart of the mother could not endure to be separated from such little children. In her desperation she determined that she would no longer hide anything from her mistress, or deceive her, but would take the children with her and frankly let Barbara Petrovna know.

In winter, in the December frost, she brought them, and late in the evening arrived at our Moscow house.

Barbara Petrovna was informed that the luggage waggons had arrived from Spasskoye.

"And Agatha?"

"She has arrived" . . . was the brief answer.

"Tell her to rest, and to-morrow morning to come and attend to my toilet."

The next morning, when Barbara Petrovna rang, Agatha went in to her.

Never, either before or since, have I seen her face so stern and determined as then, when, having kissed her mistress's hand, she stepped back a little from the bed.

"Well, so you have arrived. And what have you brought?" asked Barbara Petrovna.

Agatha silently handed her a list of all the braid, lace, and everything that had been made during the year by the embroiderers and lace makers.

Barbara Petrovna looked at it and put the paper on the table.

"Very well, you may go," and she took her cup in her hand.

Agatha took a few steps and stopped at the door.

"Go," repeated Barbara Petrovna, "I will ring."

"Madame," said Agatha, and her voice trembled, she was panting for breath.

"What's the matter with you?" asked Barbara Petrovna irritably.

"Barbara Petrovna," continued Agatha in a firmer, almost harsh voice . . . "I have brought all my children with me . . . do as you will . . . but I could not. . . ."

"What children? What is this you are telling me?"

"Madame," cried Agatha, and she fell on her knees. . . . "For God's sake let me keep them here; I will serve you as I have always served you, day and night I will be with you, only let me . . . let me know that they are here!"

"Away!" cried Barbara Petrovna.

"Do what you will with me, but I will not go away Barbara Petrovna! You had little children of your own, could they do without their mother? For God's sake, I beg you to have pity, and not take my children away!" and the poor woman, on her knees, began to crawl towards her mistress's bed.

"Away!" was the answer.

I stood there, tears pouring down my cheeks, and all I could say was: "Mamma! mamma!"

"How dare you cry! Go away!" Barbara Petrovna's anger was turned on me.

I went out, ran into the corridor and sobbed uncontrollably.

And from the bedroom came the furious cry of Barbara Petrovna, all the time becoming more violent. I went into the adjoining room.

"I can do anything I like with you, I can deport you! I can send your children to a foundling home!" . . . was heard from the bedroom.

"Whether to Siberia, or anywhere else, but with my children . . . my children, I can't . . . I won't give up my children" . . . stammered Agatha brokenly, still on her knees.

Barbara Petrovna rang the bell violently and shouted for her maids.

Two chambermaids came in.

"Take her away, take her out, drag her out!" ordered their mistress.

By then Agatha scarcely knew what she was doing, she was so beside herself with rage.

The maids took her by the hand, but she swiftly got to her feet, drawing herself away from them, and through her sobs and the agitation of the maids I heard only the words ". . . Animals . . . and their children. . . ."

"Be quiet!" cried Barbara Petrovna . . . "I command you to go. You shall rot in prison!"

"Wherever you like, but I would rather choke them with my own own hands than send them away . . . what could they do without a mother?"

"Take her to the police station! Away!" Barbara Petrovna was nearly foaming at the mouth. "What's the matter with you?"

Agatha was still standing, and the maids who had been summoned were quite petrified.

"Agatha Simonovna, let us go" . . . one of them at last whispered.

The unhappy woman made a step towards the door, then suddenly turned again towards her mistress; on her kindly face and in her beautiful eyes was a flash of anger, and she burst out in a firm, ringing voice:—

"My husband and I, Madame, have been your faithful, zealous servants, but we are not going to be forced to serve by being threatened with blows!"

Then I saw a terrible scene: Barbara Petrovna, hoarse with rage, threw herself out of bed, with one hand seized Agatha by the throat, and with the other it seemed as if she tried to tear her mouth to pieces . . . but immediately let go, and almost falling into the nearest armchair she had an attack of nerves.

Agatha remained and she and the maids laid her mistress on the bed. Doctor Porphyry Timofeyevich arrived with his laurel drops.

For a long time Barbara Petrovna sipped these drops and orange water, and at last sent for her chief clerk, Leon Ivanov (Agatha's brother-in-law, and uncle of the persecuted children).

He appeared before his mistress, his hands behind his back.

"Write this order," said Barbara Petrovna, "here !"

The clerk went out, and in a few minutes brought paper, ink and pen, and at his mistress's dictation, began to write on the chest of drawers which stood in Barbara Petrovna's bedroom, and at the present moment is before my eyes.

"*To my Moscow house office—*

An order.

"*This very day, Agatha's three children, who arrived yesterday from Spasskoye, must be sent back in the cart to Spasskoye. I command Alexander Danilov to accompany them, and to inform me at once of their arrival.*'

Then followed Barbara Petrovna's signature.

"Carry this out !" She confirmed it by word of mouth.

The clerk went out.

When Barbara Petrovna sent for me later, and she saw my red eyes, she showered reproaches on me:

"Every serf is dearer to you than your mother ! You ought to weep because they don't listen to me, they drive me to hysterics, and worry me by their disobedience, and you weep for these slaves and their slave children ! You always were, and always will be an unfeeling creature ! You are glad when they annoy me, you neither pity nor love me . . . I am ill . . . and you and your serfs ! There's no love in you, and no devotion to me at all. . . ."

Hysterics again, and again the doctor and his drops, and I was quite baffled and in despair, that my tears had again troubled mamma ; and I was sorry for Agatha, and felt as if I were in some way guilty.

At last, being driven out of the bedroom as a punishment for my ingratitude and heartlessness, I ran into the maids' room, and, on the breast of my good, kind Agatha, wept out all my grief.

And how full of love was the heart of this excellent woman ! In the midst of her own sorrow, she found words to comfort and cheer me.

The next morning, when Agatha came to dress me, in the room adjoining Barbara Petrovna's bedroom, I looked at her, and we understood each other without a word. I read the answer to my dumb question in her eyes. The children had not been sent away. She nodded her head, and pointed to the wing. I sighed with relief.

Near the Loshakovsky house at Ostozhenka, there was a large wing for the servants belonging to the estate.

Polyakov the steward, had a separate room, and in this room, in winter and spring, lived the three poor little girls, locked up, without fresh air, but all the same near their father and mother, who, in their leisure moments, were able to see them several times a day.

I often went there, I slipped away quietly from mamma to have a look at them.

They all three sat on the floor, in little pink striped cotton frocks ; near them were a few broken toys, and on each little face was a smile of pleasure at seeing me. They are all still living, and greet me with the same joyful smile, when I, though rarely, go to see them.

But there was no little trouble when the bright spring days came; the eldest girl was already a person of some understanding, and was firmly determined to go out walking. When Barbara Petrovna was asleep, they were like little animals let out of prison, but the rest of the time they were locked up, and I often heard Agatha in a fright say, " God preserve us ! They have run out ! She will see them ! "

So these poor children lived, and Barbara Petrovna never knew they were near.

Later, Ivan Sergeyevich heard of it, and it increased

his esteem for the whole family.

How the Polyakov family adored their good master is shown by their letters to me, in which they speak about every interview with him, and every letter received from him.

I went purposely to Polyakov's son, to get from him all Ivan Sergeyevich's letters, but, unfortunately, there were none to be found. The letters between the years '52 and '54 were burned by his father, and the rest by his mother, on the death of her husband.

To the day of his death, Andrew Ivanovich Polyakov possessed the Turgenev sons' most complete confidence, especially Ivan's, and Barbara Petrovna herself was fully convinced that she had no more faithful servants than his wife and himself. But this only strengthened her continual longing to tyrannize over those who were nearest and dearest to her. Of all the troubles they both endured, I have mentioned only those that the father and mother suffered with regard to their children. I will say still more about them afterwards, and about the suffering and torment that fell to their lot because of their steadfast devotion to their masters.

Chapter Five

LIFE IN MOSCOW

Now let us return to our journey to Voronezh.

Nearly at the end of August, 1840, when the doctors had decided that I could go out again after small-pox, we left Voronezh, stayed for a few days at the ruined and not yet rebuilt Spasskoye, then removed to Moscow.

There Barbara Petrovna had her own house at Samoteka, but it was so large that she decided to sell it. In the winter of 1840 she rented the Loshakovsky house in Ostozhenka Street, and there, with the exception of the summer months and two or three winters, we lived until Barbara Petrovna's death.

In 1840 I was seven years old, and at that age I began to feel for others. Already a feeling of reasoned love and sympathy for those around me had been awakened in me. Already I could understand injustice and cruelty. And there was in me a continual struggle between love for mamma, and pity for those on whom her anger fell. I wept for them all, but I never dared to show her, even by a look, the feelings that troubled me.

As far as I was concerned, I had nothing to complain of. Barbara Petrovna loved me, and they say that she spoiled me even more than she did her sons when they were children.

She dressed me splendidly, everything came from Salomon, a celebrity at that time ; my dolls and toys were the envy of my little visitors. Nicholas Sergeyevich sent me the best children's books from Petersburg. Usually the punishments inflicted for childish faults, deserved or undeserved, could not be called painful. The most cruel punishment was banishment to a corner, where there was a chair on which I had to sit for two or three hours, and sometimes more, according to my fault.

If I happened to have made mamma very angry, then she doomed me to banishment in the greenhouse, or winter garden, where I had to sit without moving all day, and for dinner I had only three courses, and was deprived of the sweet.

I was seventeen years old when Barbara Petrovna died, and my character was not then sufficiently strong for me to oppose her, or to struggle for freedom and my own way of life. How all this would have ended had she lived longer, I do not know, but, during the last year, I began to show signs of openly protesting in defence of those who were persecuted, and Barbara Petrovna could never have put up with that from anyone.

One extraordinary feature of Barbara Petrovna's character was this: if she noticed in any one of her servants any sign of independence or self-esteem, or consciousness of his worth, she endeavoured in every way to humiliate or insult him, and if, in spite of this, the one towards whom her persecution had been directed bore it meekly, then she became gracious again; if not, she rebuked him bitterly for disobedience.

In the house they had even adopted special terms for this kind of thing, it was said " the mistress is now picking a quarrel with Ivan Vassilyev" or "it was when the mistress quarrelled with Simon Petrov" or "there, you see, the mistress is beginning to nag at Peter Ivanov, he must have dared to say something to her."

One such " quarrel " happened with the butler, Simon Kirilovich Tobolev.

He was a dark, handsome man of about thirty, most dignified in appearance and manner. Because of his occupation, he, oftener than others, had occasion to discuss household affairs with his mistress.

Barbara Petrovna noticed that Simon sometimes objected and spoke to her rather boldly when she made suggestions for household purchases or for appointments for service in the house. That was enough! The mistress began to "nag at" her favourite butler. She sent for him several times a day for one thing or another, and every time she showed her displeasure, though there had been no fault on his side. But Simon was not one of the patient kind. Among the servants he was considered proud.

Seeing himself an object of persecution, Simon, though he did not say a word in his defence, yet showed by his face that he was making an effort to control himself, and all this ended very unhappily for him.

At dinner, Simon stood behind his mistress's armchair. By her knife and fork was a small carafe of water called "the mistress's water."

When Barbara Petrovna said the word "water!" it meant the well-known "I want some water" and Simon had to pour some water from the carafe. Having drawn up her plan of attack against him, Barbara Petrovna, every time she began to raise the glass to her lips, found something very wrong with the water: either it was muddy, or it was cold, or warm or it smelled.

This happened several days in succession. Simon took away the carafe of water from the table, and in a few minutes he appeared, apparently with fresh water. Barbara Petrovna drank in silence; but the next day the same thing again . . . water! again . . . no good!

Simon took away the carafe and brought fresh water.

So it happened on that memorable day. Barbara Petrovna lifted the glass to her lips, pushed it away, and turning to Simon asked:—

"What is this?"

Silence.

"I asked you what this is?"

Again silence.

"Am I never to have any decent water?" And instantly she flung the glass of water full in her butler's face. Simon turned pale, took the carafe from the table, and went out. A few minutes later he returned, and poured out water for his mistress in a clean glass.

"Now," said Barbara Petrovna, "this is something like water!" and she drank more than half a glassful.

Then Simon, pale and with trembling lips, took a few steps forward, stood in front of the icon, crossed himself with a great cross, and said:—

"As true as God is in heaven, I swear before this image that I have given you the same water. I didn't change it."

Having said this, he turned towards his mistress, and looked her straight in the face.

Child as I then was, my heart sank, because I quite understood that mamma must not be contradicted.

A few seconds of terrible silence followed.

Then Barbara Petrovna suddenly got up from her chair and said:—

"Away!" and she left the table without finishing her meal.

Everything in the house was still as death, everybody walked on tiptoe, everybody spoke in whispers, and Barbara Petrovna locked herself in her bedroom.

That was a very miserable day. I sat on a stool in the drawing room, with my dolls, and wondered what would happen. I was very fond of Simon, and very sorry for him.

And so the day passed. We drank tea without mamma, afraid even to rattle a cup or spoon. At nine o'clock they gave me my supper alone, and my governess very, very quietly murmured through the door:—

"It is nine o'clock, Madame, the little one ought to go to bed." We heard the words "Come in." I went in, went up to Barbara Petrovna and said the usual "Good night, mamma. Bless me," and having received her kiss and blessing, lay down in her bedroom, where I always slept, with the exception of a few years.

The next day, on going out, I wept bitter tears at seeing Simon in the yard.

Instead of his smart, brown frock coat, with bright buttons, Simon had on a garment of coarse grey woollen cloth, and in his hands was a broom with which he was sweeping the yard.

By his mistress's orders he had been transformed into a handyman, and so he remained for three or four years, until he was replaced by the well-known dumb porter Andrew, who, quite by chance, was put on Barbara Petrovna's list of servants. He appears in *Mumu* under the name Gerasim.

Barbara Petrovna spent the winters of 1840 and 1841 in Moscow, cultivating her acquaintances. She had special days and evenings for receptions, and sometimes she went out in the evening to play cards with her friends.

Her son, Nicholas Sergeyevich used to come to Petersburg to stay with his mother, but I strongly suspect it was his love for Anna Yakovlevna Schwartz who still lived with us, that drew him to Moscow. Barbara Petrovna, who missed nothing, saw it all but attached no importance to it. Her son, of course, never dared to think of asking her consent to his marriage. Suddenly, in the winter of 1841, Anna Yakovlevna disappeared.

How it happened, no-one knew, or if they did, they dared not say.

Barbara Petrovna was not even surprised, and never inquired about her; but from that time, she finally ceased sending money to her son for his support in his regiment.

Nicholas Sergeyevich resigned the service, and entered the Ministry of Home Affairs under Perevsky.[1] At first his salary was sufficient for his household, but when his son was born, and within a year, a daughter, and Anna Yakovlevna was very ill, they could barely exist on his means. Nicholas Sergeyevich was forced to look for some kind of work ; he gave French lessons, and that considerably added to his income.

His mother continued to correspond with him, but to all his timid requests for assistance, she always maintained an obstinate silence.

How she knew that her son was supporting a family, we did not know for a long time; but she was fully convinced that they were not married, and hoped that their love would grow cold, and that her son would, in time, make a desirable match.

These hopes were expressed in that same album which I have preserved. Here is what I found in it : —

"A mon fils, Nicholas.

" Cher enfant, il court un bruit sur toi qui me cause un poignant chagrin. Vous avez pu vous laisser entrainer à un coupable penchant.

" Mon enfant, ne comptez pas sur les promesses des passions; elles s'évanouissent, et avec elles les serments, qui furent faits de bonne foi. S'il en est temps encore, renoncez à une faiblesse cui ne peut que vous entrainer a votre ruine. Je ne vous connais pas;[2] vous si raisonable, vous qui connaissez si bien les devoirs de la société et du rang où vous êtes placé."

---

[1] L. A. Count, Minister of the Interior. 1792-1856.
[2] Perhaps : reconnais.

Chapter Six

IVAN THE FAVOURITE SON

In 1841 Ivan Sergeyevich returned from abroad, and came for the summer to Spasskoye. There he brought his first work *Parasha*.

This did not make any great impression on us. The little book in its blue binding lay on one of the tables in his mother's study, but, as far as I remember, she did not talk much about it. The only extract quoted was taken from the words spoken somewhere: "In well ordered houses kvass is not drunk."

In consequence of these words, kvass was banished from the table, to the great grief and distress of my esteemed governess, Katherine Yegorovna Ritter, who wanted to ask to taste kvass, but no-one dared to ask Barbara Petrovna, but later it was served in the side building, where my governesses were lodged.

Barbara Petrovna's joy at meeting her son was great, though she did not compel anyone else to celebrate his home-coming. But she herself changed quite suddenly; she showed no capriciousness, no nagging, no temper.

How can this be explained except by the charm and kindness of Ivan Sergeyevich, poured out on all who surrounded him? Everybody loved him, everybody felt that he belonged to them, everybody in his heart was devoted to him, believing in his goodness, which, however, in his mother's house, could not be openly shown in anyone's defence. Nevertheless, when he arrived, they said "Our angel, our defender is here."

Knowing his mother's character, he never spoke harshly to her about any of her actions that grieved him; he knew that it would only mean more trouble for anyone in whose defence he spoke ; yet in spite of this, Barbara Petrovna, in his presence, and for him, became quite transformed : she, who was afraid of no-one, who never adapted herself to anyone, endeavoured, for his sake, to show herself kind and tolerant.

Ivan Sergeyevich's coolness towards his mother came later . . . slowly. But it can hardly be called coolness. He simply stayed away from her. It was impossible to argue, it would have made things worse. . . . But to see and be silent was too much for his kind heart.

On his arrival from Berlin, he was unusually gentle with his mother; he had not yet managed to investigate all that happened in the house, but former things, on account of his three years' absence, he blotted out of his kindhearted memory.

Those little attentions to each other, that express most of all agreement and friendship in families, were mutual. Barbara Petrovna was thinking the whole day of how she could please her son. She ordered his favourite dishes to be prepared. Jams, especially gooseberry, of which he was very fond, were sent in large jars to his wing, and to tell the truth, they quickly disappeared, with my help, and that of sundry children belonging to the household servants, who ventured to come to the window of his wing. To them, the young master was "their man." In addition to this, Barbara Petrovna, who could not endure dogs, allowed Napli, the predecessor of the well-known Dianka, to be continually on the balcony, simply because he was Vanya's dog, and she even deigned to feed Napli with sweets from her own hand.

On his side, Ivan Sergeyevich often put off hunting, of which he was very fond, to stay with his mother, and when she expressed a wish to be wheeled in her chair round the garden (she could not walk), her son would not allow a servant to push the chair, he always did it himself.

One of the evenings of this summer was especially remarkable. That morning Ivan Sergeyevich had gone hunting, and at seven o'clock in the evening, mamma went alone in the carriage to inspect the fields. She was accompanied only by the farm bailiff on horseback. At nine o'clock a terrible storm burst, one of the worst that anyone could remember.

I hid in the darkest corner of the drawing room, and cried, because everything in the house was in dreadful confusion. There was no mistress, and no young master and no-one knew where they were.

Ivan Sergeyevich arrived first.

He changed his clothes in the wing, and then came into the house, not knowing that his mother was not there.

Seeing my tears and not knowing the cause, he began to reproach me for being afraid of thunder. As a child that really was true of me, and Ivan Sergeyevich always scolded me for it. He took me on his knee, sat down near the window, and tried to reason me out of this fear, turning my attention to the beauty of the clouds, and all nature in the storm.

This time, when in answer to his affectionate words, I began to cry out still more loudly—" The thunderstorm has killed mamma, the thunderstorm has killed mamma " —he could not for a long time understand my broken words.

" Where is mamma? " he turned to someone.

"The mistress has not returned. She went for a drive and has not returned. They have been looking for her everywhere on horseback," was the answer.

Ivan Sergeyevich rushed out of the room.

In spite of the rain, and the storm, and without putting

on a coat, he ran to the stables, seized the first horse he came across, and rode out of the gate, not knowing where: but soon he was met by the bailiff, whom Barbara Petrovna had sent home, with the order that no-one was to look for her, and the news that she was safe in the forester's hut.

Having surveyed the fields, she had decided to go into the forest, where the thunderstorm had overtaken her.

For a long, long time this weary waiting lasted: at last we heard the sound of wheels. Ivan Sergeyevich ran to the balcony, carried his mother from the carriage and put her in her chair, and felt her dress and legs.

"Are you not wet through, mamma?" . . . he was very much upset, and kept kissing her hands. . . . "Well, thank God, thank God" . . . he repeated, "that nothing has happened to you, for I was so afraid for you; the horses might have taken fright and bolted; that thought was never out of my head."

And again he embraced his mother and kissed her.

Such were the relations between son and mother . . . and it was sad and grievous to see how they changed later.

To me, personally, Ivan Sergeyevich's arrival meant much. Apart from the happiness of seeing him whom I adored, there were many other reasons for rejoicing.

To begin with, all lessons were discontinued; he maintained that lessons were harmful for children in summer. He would take my part openly, whether I was reprimanded deservedly or undeservedly, and often from Barbara Petrovna's lips was heard the good natured "You are spoiling the little one." But our best time of all was after dinner, when mamma went to her bedroom to rest.

Ivan Sergeyevich then lay down on the *pâté*.

I do not think that such a piece of furniture can be met with anywhere now, but then, at Spasskoye, this square structure, with fantastic arabesques embroidered on canvas, occupied the whole of the centre of the small drawing room in the new house.

And on this piece of furniture Ivan Sergeyevich would lie, though his legs didn't fit on it, and indeed about a yard and a half of him stretched out into space, and I sat by him, and we told stories.

However, it was I and not he who did the talking. And to this day I cannot understand why I did not bore him with my oft repeated one and the same story, my then favourite: "The blue pheasant." Sometimes I told him others, but he, having noticed that I really liked this one better than the others, even pretended (so I thought afterwards) that he liked it himself, and that he had forgotten some of the details. And all this to give pleasure to a child!

But besides establishing ourselves on the familiar *pâté* we sometimes made plundering raids on the grocery cupboard.

At Spasskoye this cupboard had a historic tradition.

Adjoining the house was a gallery built of stone, left untouched by the fire: the library was put there, and on the left side, near the entrance, stood an immense cupboard, in charge of the old footman of Ivan Sergeyevich's late father.

Michael Philipovich, as he was called, was pensioned off on the death of his master. So that he might have some little thing to do, the keys of the library and the cupboard were handed over to him.

Mentioning the library, I may say that Ivan Sergeyevich, in saying that his first acquaintance with Russian literature was through his mother's personal attendant, was probably speaking about this same Michael Philipovich, because when I was a little older, I often, of course unknown to mamma, went to ask the old man for French books to read; he would wave his hands despairingly, his accustomed gesture, and say:—

'Why, young lady, why do you read these French books? What is there in them? Now you should read Kheraskov.[1] That really is a good book."

But then I thought nothing better than Mme. de Genlis, and translations of Mrs. Radcliffe.

Michael was very deaf, and although at that time we did not notice it, rather queer. His peculiarities, his character, and afterwards his tragic death, proved this.

His madness came on gradually, in consequence of his deafness and his desire for solitude after his master's death. It was evident that he had gone through so much that it had secretly embittered his soul. It seems that he became deaf on the 14th of December, 1825,[2] following shell shock. He would sometimes say how and why, in a whisper and halting words. One conversation of which I was a witness, proved the truth of this assumption.

The late Sergius Nikoleyevich Turgenev had a friend and fellow officer, Rodion Yegorovich Grünwald; his portrait and biography appeared in *World Illustrated* 1877 (pages 92-95). Grünwald then and afterwards was always a friend of the Turgenev family. In my time he came about four times from Petersburg to Spasskoye, nearly always in September, because he was passionately fond of hunting. He stayed a week or more with us at Spasskoye. Barbara Petrovna did everything possible to entertain and amuse her valued guest. She herself followed the hunt in her carriage; at chosen spots she waited for the huntsmen, and for those neighbours who had been invited to a luxurious lunch; there were other entertainments also.

[1] M. M. Kheraskov, Poet. 1733-1807.
[2] So-called Decembrists' rising.

During one, of his visits, Grünwald went with Barbara Petrovna to the library.

Michael Philipovich stood up, and something came over his face; not a smile, because nobody ever saw him smile, but a kind of glow.

" Well, old man, and how are you?" . . . the General turned to him.

" Just getting along, Your Excellency, but I have become very deaf. I can't hear anything."

"He has been deaf since the 14th. You remember:" interposed Barbara Petrovna.

"Well, old man, we've gone through a lot together," the General shouted in the old man's ear.

"Yes, yes, Your Excellency. What a terrible lot of firing there was!"

The conversation stopped there, but it was evident that Grünwald, Barbara Petrovna and the old man thoroughly understood each other.

The fact was that Michael Philipovich's deafness was so great that, having gradually got out of the habit of listening, he rarely spoke himself, lived alone, continually read religious books, and being entirely left to himself, had one fixed idea, the object of his care . . . . the grocery cupboard. To him it was the most precious of his mistress's possessions. . . . to the young servants an object of amusement, and to me. . . . the promised land flowing with milk and honey. It contained everything that could be found in a good shop.

Everything was bought in large quantities at Andreyev's,[1] brought from Moscow and handed over to Michael Philipovich. His stinginess was extraordinary. Having received all the purchases, he would sigh heavily, and dramatically shake his head.

[1] Famous Moscow grocery.

"And why have they brought such a lot," he would say. "No matter how much they bring it will all be eaten!"

Every morning the cook would go to him, and ask for the things that she wanted from the cupboard.

With a sigh the old man would weigh out everything, and hand it over, and, if half a pound of anything was wanted, and he found after weighing, even a few grains or a pinch of anything over, for his own satisfaction he would put it back.

When, to his dismay, there were visitors and quantities of provisions were needed, Michael Philipovich sighed so loudly, and waved his hands in such horror, that on such days, I, as well as others, went to gaze at his despair, as if it were a show. We did not know then that it really was torture to him.

Every day, after dinner, I got permission to go to Michael Philipovich, and every time I was told how much and what to get.

"Mamma has ordered five prunes, or two dried figs," I would call out solemnly.

Then the old man would push his glasses up on his forehead, and look suspiciously at me for a long, long time, then he would appear to be looking for the key, and at last he would, not open, but only half open the cupboard, because my predatory fingers were always trying to filtch something, not so much because I wanted the dainties, as just to tease the old man; then he would clutch his head in despair, and quickly, only just avoiding shutting me in to it, he would try to close the cupboard, and would helplessly whisper :—

"I will tell mamma . . . I will tell mamma."

He always went to bed early, on a broad wooden bench near the cupboard. But he did not sleep peacefully, because often in the evening some of the young servants would make a noise on purpose, and rattle the keys near him. But deaf as was this guardian of his mistress's property, he would jump up, and in indescribable terror look round ; but, of course, there was never anybody to be found. I think that even Ivan Sergeyevich's arrival was not a joy to Michael Philipovich.

With the words " let us go and rummage," we would go to the cupboard. Sometimes Ivan assumed a ferocious aspect, walking with unusually prancing steps, while I, holding him by the hand, followed almost at a run, and so it happened that we would come face to face with the Spasskoye Harpagon.[1]

" Open ! " Ivan Sergeyevich would say.

For him, grown up and undoubted master, the cupboard was opened wide, and he authoritatively rummaged about in it.

At first the old man would lean his cheek on his hand, and sigh, and sigh deeply.

I was delighted, and held Ivan Sergeyevich by the sleeve, and nodded towards the old man. Ivan Sergeyevich would look sideways at him, and continue to lay waste the upper shelf, and I, a little more timidly, the lower.

Michael Philipovich would shake his head, and wave his hands. We were all the more delighted.

At last the old man could endure it no longer. He approached, rattling his keys, and even made a movement as if to close the cupboard.

" Wait, wait, Michael Philipovich," said his master soothingly, " I haven't finished yet."

I wasn't eating now. I was in convulsions of laughter. And so it went on ; the old man would wait, and wait

[1] Molicre's *L'avare*.

until we had eaten our fill, and at last in an imploring voice he would say: —

"Sir! Have pity on mamma! Really, you will have stomach ache!"

After a few days of such raids, Michael Philipovich would appear before his mistress.

First of all, as he was privileged to do, he kissed her hand.

"Well, what is it?" Barbara Petrovna would ask, knowing of old that some complaint would follow.

"Madame, there's nothing! There's nothing left!"

"What do you mean by nothing?"

"Just that, Madame, nothing! . . ." he waved his hands. "There's nothing left. They've eaten it all up!"

"Well then," his mistress quietly and with a smile consoled him, "write out a list of what you want, and send the carrier into Mtsensk or Orel for it."

"But indeed, they've eaten it all up!" the old man would repeat emphatically and despairingly.

Barbara Petrovna would laugh. And Michael Philipovich, not finding her sympathetic, would stand for a while, sigh, and go away.

The poor old man's death was tragic. About two years after Barbara Petrovna's death, my Agatha, then a freed-woman, came and told me that Michael Philipovich had hanged himself in the attic of the Spasskoye house.

A few days afterwards I was dining with the Nicholas Sergeyevichs, when, in answer to my question about the terrible death of the poor old man, Nicholas Sergeyevich said: —

"You remember Michael Philipovich's stinginess, at which we all used to laugh. It must have been a kind of madness, because after mamma's death, seeing a new order at Spasskoye, all the expenditure of money, and, in his opinion, waste of goods (*et vous savez que Jean n'y va pas de main morte quand il s'agit de dépenses*) . . . seeing all this, the old man became more and more thoughtful and worried, continually affirming: 'The young people will have to go begging, they will have to beg all over the world ! ' He couldn't endure it, and so he committed suicide."

What troubled the old man most of all were the presents showered by Ivan Sergeyevich on his mother's former servants. Ivan Sergeyevich gave both money and land, allotted pensions, and to Michael Philipovich himself gave a private and more convenient dwelling . . . but all this only increased the old man's despair.

"Soon, our serfs will be living better than their masters," said the old man. "Then what will be left for the masters ? "

Speaking about the gratuities so generously bestowed by Ivan Sergeyevich, I must say that his kindheartedness carried him away, and that he sometimes gave to the unworthy ; but there were some who had undoubtedly earned their reward for long endurance under his mother's yoke.

Among such was Barbara Petrovna's doctor, Porphyry Timofeyevich Kergashev.

The first time Ivan Sergeyevich went to Berlin, Porphyry was sent with him, as a kind of *valet-de chambre* or, rather, tutor. Since then, the relations between him and his master had always been cordial. When Ivan Sergeyevich was with us, we often saw them together having a most friendly conversation, and no-one ever thought it strange, because for her sons, for me and everyone else, Porphyry Timofeyevich was a doctor and a favourite ; Barbara Petrovna alone looked upon him as a serf.

To all Ivan Sergeyevich's requests that she should give Porphyry his freedom, she never consented; nevertheless, of all her serfs, he was the only one whom Barbara Petrovna never insulted, either by word or deed, and sometimes she had even more faith in him than in her own best physicians.

In all his mistress's difficult moments of life, in all her attacks of real or fancied illness, Porphyry appeared with his unfailing laurel drops, and the inevitable words: " Please, Madame, calm yourself."

And indeed it seemed as if one look at this calm and sturdy figure was enough to soothe every nerve. The outward appearance of our dear doctor was typical: he was tall and solidly built, with a trace of small-pox on his face, which did not at all detract from his kindhearted expression; remarkably small eyes in comparison with his colossal stature, but very bright and kindly. His whole body breathed a serene calm. Barbara Petrovna called it phlegm . . . *toujours endormi* . . . but for all that, she felt at rest only when he was there.

The years that Porphyry Timofeyevich spent in Berlin were not unfruitful. There, he finally learnt to speak German quite fluently, and, having for a short time attended the school for hospital orderlies in Russia, he went to lectures of the medical faculty in Berlin, and left as a fairly experienced doctor. On returning to Russia, Porphyry Timofeyevich continued to read and employ himself. His mistress never grudged money for his books.

In Moscow, Barbara Petrovna's friend and family doctor never prescribed any treatment or undertook any case in the house without first talking it over with Porphyry Timofeyevich and getting his opinion.

Theodore Ivanovich Inozemtsev himself, who began to

treat Barbara Petrovna in '48, took an interest in him, recognized his knowledge and outstanding ability, and allowed him, with the rest of his students, to be present every morning when the patients were brought in, and, on an equal footing with the others, to hear his diagnosis of their complaints. In this manner, Porphyry's experience was enriched by the words of our celebrated doctor.

At Spasskoye, Porphyry Timofeyevich's fame spread far beyond the borders of the Mtsensk district. Squires sent their carriages for him, but, alas, as a serf he could go only when his mistress permitted it.

And no matter how often Ivan Sergeyevich begged his mother to give him his freedom, he always got a refusal, after which followed the enumeration of all the favours and privileges that his favourite enjoyed, and that, in her opinion, were quite enough to distinguish him from the rest of the servants; he had his own room, almost a study, in the house itself ; his food was sent from the family table ; he received four times as much as the others in wages ; and, in Moscow, he could even leave the house without asking permission.

" All that is very good," said Ivan Sergeyevich, " but why not take this yoke from him ? I promise you that he will never leave you as long as you live. Only give him the knowledge that he is a man, not a slave, a thing that you can send where and when you will, according to your wish or whim."

But his mother remained inexorable. Porphyry Timofeyevich received his freedom from her sons, on their mother's death.

But he did not leave his beloved master ; he settled first at Spasskoye, and worked there among the sick, then, having passed an examination, he became a country medical officer at Mtsensk.

I made inquiries about his later fortunes, and learned that he was seriously ill for a long time. Ivan Sergeyevich took him again to Spasskoye, and surrounded him with the utmost care and attention until his death.

Only once did he come in painful contact with his mistress. Even then his calmness did not fail him. A remarkable example of courage and confidence in himself was shown by this serf, who was not even intimidated by Barbara Petrovna's terrible anger.

I was ten years old when I fell ill with fever. It was at Spasskoye. Mamma was in despair. At first Porphyry Timofeyevich was treating me, but seeing that my condition was becoming worse, Barbara Petrovna wanted to send to Mtsensk for doctors, and to Orel for Gutzeit. But Porphyry Timofeyevich would not consent.

Serenely calm, and with his rather rolling walk, he entered his mistress's room, just when she had written a letter sending for Gutzeit.

"There is no need, Madame, to upset yourself and send for anyone at all; I have begun to treat the young mistress, and I will cure her."

Barbara Petrovna darted a look at him . . . pushed the letter aside, looked searchingly at this bold fellow, and said: —

"Remember! If you don't cure her . . . Siberia ! "

But that did not worry our dear doctor. Slowly and calmly as usual he went out of the room, sat near my bed, and never left me, day or night, until the crisis had passed.

Then, in that same stolid manner, expressing neither triumph nor joy (although he was very fond of me) he entered that same room where he had been threatened with Siberia, and announced: —

"Now the young lady will live, but her recovery will be slow."

Chapter Seven

FAMILY VIEWS AND A FAMILY TRAGEDY

IVAN SERGEYEVICH'S entry into the field of literature did not please Barbara Petrovna.

There were often conversations about it between mother and son. Once we were sitting on the balcony at Spass-koye ; Barbara Petrovna and I, with Ivan Sergeyevich, at whose feet lay his well-known Dianka, who was the successor of his former dog, Napli.

Ivan Sergeyevich was very jolly, and was telling his mother how Michael Philipovich had advised him to eat less, and he was talking about Pushkin's *Avaricious Knight*.

Suddenly, Ivan Sergeyevich jumped up, and with quick steps walked along the balcony.

"Ah! If only I had Pushkin's talent!" he cried regretfully. "Wouldn't I make a poem about Michael Philipovich! Ah! What talent! But what am I? Perhaps I shall never write anything good in all my life."

"But I can't understand," said Barbara Petrovna almost contemptuously, "why you are so anxious to be an author. Is that a profession suitable for a squire? You say yourself that you won't be a Pushkin . . . and as for such verses as his, that is permissible. But a writer! For goodness sake what is a writer? In my opinion there's no difference between an author and a quill-driver. They both scribble for money. . . . You are a squire, and you ought to serve the State, and make a career and a name for yourself, but not by scribbling. And in any case, who reads Russian books? If only you would enter a regular service, obtain rank and distinction, and then marry, for you are now the only one to prevent the Turgenev family from dying out."

Ivan Sergeyevich answered his mother's exhortation with jokes, but when it was a question of his marriage, he burst into a fit of laughter : —

" As for that, mamma, excuse me, but don't expect it ! I shall not marry ! Sooner than that your Spasskoye church with its two crosses would begin to dance a jig."

At these words, I couldn't control myself, but burst out laughing.

" How dare you laugh when he talks rubbish ! " cried Barbara Petrovna. " And, Jean," she turned to her son, " how can you talk such nonsense before a child ! "

But all day afterwards, I couldn't look at Ivan Sergeyevich without laughing.

" And I can't understand," continued Ivan Sergeyevich, " why you, mamma, talk so scornfully about authors . . . there was a time when all you ladies ran after Pushkin . . . and you yourself liked and respected Zhukovsky."

" Ah ! That's quite another thing . . . Zhukovsky, who wouldn't have admired him . . . you know what a favourite he was at Court ! "

The following shows still more clearly Barbara Petrovna's opinion of Russian literature.

She at last deigned to read *Dead Souls*.

" It's frightfully amusing ! " she praised it in Russian, " but to tell the truth, I have never read anything in worse taste or more improper," she finished in French.

Between 1841 and 1846 Ivan Sergeyevich was at Spasskoye every summer, but in winter he often went to Moscow to his mother ; here the friend who visited him most was the late Timofey Nikolayevich Granovsky.[1]

Ivan Sergeyevich occupied a room in the upper storey.

[1] Russian Historian, leader of the Westernisers. Professor of History, 1813-1855.

I was always allowed free access to him, and I always ran there when mamma was resting, or when she was busy with visitors. Granovsky always treated me kindly. Once I went upstairs when both of them, host and guest, were talking very loudly. Ivan Sergeyevich was walking rapidly up and down the room, and was apparently becoming very much excited. I stopped at the door. Granovsky beckoned me to him and seated me on his knee. I sat there for a long time, holding my breath, and, at first, I did not understand anything ; but at the words: serfs, free, exile, misfortune, when will it end, etc., words well known to me and often heard, their conversation became comprehensible ; I could not then or now give an exact account of all that I heard, but the meaning was clear. In their conversation they so emphatically expressed a hope for something better that I was overjoyed.

Suddenly Ivan Sergeyevich, as if coming to himself, remembered me, and turned to me:—

"You are sleepy, get down, you don't understand anything about this ; it's time for you to go to bed."

"Don't I understand ! " I was insulted. "Isn't it that my Agatha will soon be freed ? "

"Yes, some time," said Ivan Sergeyevich thoughtfully, and at this he kissed me as if pleased with me.

During one of these winters Liszt came to Moscow.

He gave one of his concerts, not in the concert hall belonging to the nobility, but in someone's private house.

Barbara Petrovna, who very rarely went out, wanted, however, to hear the great artist. Ivan Sergeyevich went with her. The stairs leading to the concert hall were steep, and the carrying-chair, on which the servants usually carried her upstairs, had not been brought. Barbara Petrovna's legs were at that time weak and swollen ; to climb so high was not to be thought of. Barbara

Petrovna's eyes blazed with anger at the careless servants.

"I will carry you, mamma," said Ivan Sergeyevich, and, not waiting for his mother's assent or objection, at once seized her in his arms like a child, carried her up the stairs, and put her down near the entrance to the hall. Many of the public witnessed this scene.

There was a whisper of surprise and sympathy. There were many who came to Barbara Petrovna and congratulated her on the happiness of having such an attentive and affectionate son.

Perhaps she was pleased herself, for the servants were not rebuked for the forgotten chair.

That year Ivan Sergeyevich was much troubled with his eyes. The pupils were so contracted that sometimes they could hardly be seen. He was having treatment, and for bathing the eyes some kind of green liquid was used.

Every afternoon he lay on the divan. I put the towels on, and so my afternoon sittings with him were resumed; but I no longer told him tales of the blue pheasant. Ivan Sergeyevich was not cheerful. We spoke quietly about Agatha, about her children, and of how everybody was afraid of mamma; I told him my childish griefs, and those of others, and often quite innocently leaned on his breast. He often sighed at my stories, and was visibly distressed; but I did not understand then that what grieved him was his complete inability to help anyone, with a child's cruel egoism, I rejoiced that he shared my sorrows. I never dared to tell anything to anyone else. I was afraid of several of my governesses, and I did not trust them—because they might very well have reported me to mamma, and I got into trouble often enough on account of those "slaves" without this.

Ivan Sergeyevich's opinions about my lessons were very original.

Usually, when he arrived, he heard accounts of my progress in learning, and excellence in languages, as if it was something unusual.

Once Barbara Petrovna praised my knowledge of French.

"I believe it, I believe it," he answered, "she chatters very well, certainly."

"And she writes without any mistakes," added mamma.

"Now I won't believe that; because as regards the ending of the participles, she really isn't up to much. But you are not the only one," he comforted me. "All Russian ladies and girls are in the same boat. Everything goes smoothly until you reach a participle, and that's the end of it! Somewhere there's a superfluous s or an e missing."

Another time, I was then about twelve years old, I had taken up English. I already spoke French and German well, and indeed learned to speak English in a very short time.

Ivan Sergeyevich arrived. Again my copy books were shown to him, and again my success was praised.

But my progress was the one thing that Ivan Sergeyevich treated with irony. He saw only my outward drawing-room education, which was principally founded on a knowledge of languages.

One morning before Barbara Petrovna had left her bedroom, and before I had started my lessons, a mischievous fit came over me; I chattered continuously, and could not sit still in one place. My good Miss Blackwood did not know what to do with me.

Suddenly, from the gallery just above my desk, Ivan Sergeyevich's voice resounded:—

"And they have praised your success, but I tell you that, although you can chatter English, there are two

very important phrases you do not know: ' Be quiet '
and ' hold your tongue.' "

And I was quiet!

He often joked about my piano playing ; every morning I had to play scales.

Once, when he had listened long enough, Ivan Sergeyevich expressed himself thus : —

" I like to hear your scales. The first flows along like
a swift stream on a smooth bed, not one stone to hinder
it. The second represents a rugged river bed. The third
meets stones . . . the fourth and fifth run over boulders,
and F major is just like the Dnieper rapids."[1]

With what pleasure do I always remember his good-
natured jokes about learning and talents, and how affec-
tionately do I treasure every word of his in my memory!

In 1879, the year of the Pushkin celebrations, in one
of my letters to him, I reminded him of all this, and
finally set his mind at rest about the participles, and
affirmed that after long teaching experience I had
" acquired this wisdom." At our last meeting, he laughed
very much at this comment.

In 1846, before Ivan Sergeyevich's departure abroad,
Madame Viardot came to Moscow.

She gave a concert. Barbara Petrovna already knew of
her son's attachment to the Viardot family, and, of course,
did not like it, but she went to hear the artist. The concert was a morning one. On arriving home, she was very
much annoyed because Ivan Sergeyevich did not return
for dinner. All the time she sat frowning, and never
said a word. At the end of the meal, she banged her
knife angrily on the table, and, as if talking to herself
and not referring to anyone, she said : —

" One must confess that that cursed gipsy sings
well!"[2]

[1] Nearly word for word. His own comparison.
[2] Her own words.

In the summer of 1845, Barbara Petrovna went to Petersburg with the intention of preventing her elder son's marriage with Anna Yakovlevna Schwartz (it had already taken place secretly some time before). From letters which I have kept, I see that she was there from the 1st of June to the 23rd of July of that year.

Until now I have not said anything about Nicholas Sergeyevich, Ivan's elder brother.

Just as Ivan Sergeyevich's outward appearance, distinguished as it was, was purely Russian, so Nicholas's was rather that of an English than a Russian gentleman.

When I read *Jane Eyre*, a novel very popular at that time, I imagined Rochester as being just like Nicholas Sergeyevich. And I was not the only one. Many others gave him this nickname.

The brothers were always great friends. But the difference in their characters was immense. I am speaking, of course, about them in their home life.

Ivan Sergeyevich was distinguished for his unusual kindheartedness and harmless humour.

Nicholas Sergeyevich was sarcastic, and although there was no evil in him, he was occasionally inclined to wound, and even laugh satirically at people.

Ivan Sergeyevich would look for an opportunity of doing good. Nicholas Sergeyevich would not refuse to do it if an opportunity presented itself, or if requested.

And it is pleasant to remember that after his mother's death, Nicholas Sergeyevich was always very good to me.

Ivan Sergeyevich's speech was not quite smooth ; he lisped a little, and sometimes, as it were, had to search for an expression, but it was always kindly ; a certain cordiality showed in all his words ; his voice was unusually gentle and sympathetic, and when he became excited, rather shrill, but never harsh. Once having heard it one never forgot it.

Nicholas Sergeyevich's speech was unusually florid and sonorous. I have never heard anyone else speak in that way in any language.

He was an excellent *ranconteur*. He knew several languages thoroughly, and pronounced every one as well as he pronounced his own.

It is said that we Russians are unusually capable of acquiring a correct, pure pronunciation of foreign languages, but not many attain such perfection as Nicholas Sergeyevich. And the most remarkable thing was, that it was without any affectation.

Often I happened to listen to him. His periods were purely classical in length. In his stories he sometimes brought in a number of episodes and anecdotes, but all these digressions had a definite connection with the whole; he never lost the thread, and did not cause his hearers to go astray in the labyrinth of his brilliant oratory.

No matter how much or how long he spoke, we were surprised and delighted by his remarkable gift of presenting everything so pictorially and vividly. Some of his longest stories were full of humorous, as well as rather sarcastic and sparkling wit, and when he was silent, we always wanted to say, "Oh! do go on ! "

More than once Barbara Petrovna said: "I made a mistake in my sons' names. I ought to have called Nicholas Ivan. He is my John Chrysostom (golden voiced).

I must say, however, that Nicholas Sergeyevich was only eloquent and friendly in his own family, and with very close friends.

In society, and especially the society of women, I have never seen anyone duller, or more intolerable.

Silent, with a sarcastic smile on his lips ; awkward and extremely confused in manner ; that is how society saw him.

So Barbara Petrovna went to Petersburg. She was firmly convinced that Nicholas was not married, though rumours had reached her that he had some children.

She wanted to see them, but she wouldn't have them in the house, so she ordered them to be brought into the street, and led past her windows, and this was done.

Their grandmother looked at them through her lorgnette, and remarked that the eldest boy reminded her of Nicholas Sergeyevich as a child, and that was all that she ever said about the children.

In order to persuade him to break off what she then supposed was his connection with Anna Yakovlevna, Barbara Petrovna begged him to go to Spasskoye, and look after all her estates, because she was not then on very good terms with her brother-in-law, Nicholas Nikolayevich, and she promised him wonderful things ; but Nicholas firmly refused, and explained to his mother that he could not abandon his family. So he stayed on in Petersburg, and by his service, and lessons, he kept his family until 1849, when, at last, Barbara Petrovna consented to his marriage.

A great sorrow befell Nicholas Sergeyevich and his wife. One winter all their three children died, and no more were born to them afterwards.

Once I had a very sad interview with Nicholas Sergeyevich. I was then married, and we had not seen each other for a long time ; sitting in the studio of his Prechistensky house,[1] I was talking to him about my life, my family and my little daughter, and when I told him of my fear of losing her, he suddenly got up and recited to me Victor Hugo's well-known poem: *Lorsque l'enfant paraît*. When he came to the last lines:

---

[1] A street in Moscow.

Seigneur, préservez moi, préservez ceux que j'aime
Frères, parents, amis ; et mes ennemis même
Dans le mal triomphants,
  De voir jamais, Seigneur, l'été sans fleurs vermeilles,
  Le cage sans oiseaux, la ruche sans abeilles,
La maison sans enfants. [1]

he wept bitterly, almost sobbed.

I was very sorry that by my conversation I had awakened his unhappy memory of his own dead children. When he grew a little calmer, Nicholas Sergeyevich began to tell me what he had suffered at that time ; he spoke of his little ones' last days and words, and ended by saying : —

"On dirait que c'est la malédiction de maman qui a amené mes enfants au tombeau."

At that moment an episode relating to his children's portraits came back to my memory, and in my turn I related it to him.

On arriving home from Petersburg, Barbara Petrovna took a fancy to ask her son for his children's portraits.

Seeing in this, as he confessed afterwards, a glimmer of tenderness, and even building a little hope on it, Nicholas Sergeyevich was not long in carrying out his mother's order.

The portraits were taken, and sent by post to Moscow.

Notice of their despatch was sent from Petersburg. Barbara Petrovna signed the form for their receipt, and the following morning ordered them to be brought to her in her bedroom.

[1] Oh God! Bless me and mine and those I love
  And e'en my foes that still triumphant prove
    Victors by force or guile.
  A flowerless summer may we never see
  Or nest of birds bereft, or hive of bee
    Or home of infant's smile.
            L. G. Bell & Sons, New York. 1887.
            The translation by Harry Highton, M.A.

Andrew Ivanovich took in the little box which was sewn up in linen.

"Cut it, and open it," was the order.

Polyakov did so, took out several sheets of paper which were folded on top, and had scarcely had time to lift out the first portrait in its frame, when Barbara Petrovna said:—

"Give it to me!"

The box was handed over and put on a table in front of her.

"Go!... Shut the door."

I stood in the adjoining room with Agatha, holding my breath... what was going to happen?

I must say in passing that we all in the house, always knew, by the first word that Barbara Petrovna said on awakening, what sort of mood she was in, and what sort of a day we should have.

This time everything foretold a storm, and we awaited it in terror.

In a little while, we heard a noise as of some object being thrown on the floor, and the sound of flying pieces of glass.

Then again some sort of banging on glass, and something violently thrown on the floor, then silence.

Of course we guessed that the children's portraits had been thrown down and smashed.

"Agatha!" burst out Barbara Petrovna's stern voice.

Agatha went in. Her mistress pointed to the floor....

"Sweep it up and see that no glass is left on the carpet. Then put the box down on the table."

"Throw it out," she added

That same winter all three children died.

Neither before nor since, except for what I have told here, did Barbara Petrovna ever mention Nicholas Sergeyevich's family, and he never made any attempt to soften his mother's heart towards her grandchildren. He knew his mother too well not to understand the uselessness of pleas and reminders of his poor little ones.

Chapter Eight

THE DUMB GIANT

OVER every episode of my life spent with Barbara Petrovna which I have undertaken to describe, lies a sad, even a painful shadow. But such was all our life. There was very little sunshine.

Who has not read *Mumu*? Who is not acquainted with her owner Gerasim? Ivan Sergeyevich's whole story about these two unfortunate beings is not fictitious. All this unhappy drama took place before my eyes, and I hope that a few details of how Gerasim, or rather, the dumb Andrew, came to be with us, will not be without interest.

Nearly every summer Barbara Petrovna made a tour of inspection, that is, she undertook long journeys to her estates in the provinces of Orel, Tula, and Kursk.

With special pleasure do I remember these journeys, which were usually carried out in a number of vehicles. There was Barbara Petrovna's own carriage, a barouche containing my governess and the chief chambermaid, a covered cart for the doctor, a cart for the laundry maid and my maid, and a waggon for the cook and kitchen.

These journeys were prolonged, and sometimes lasted whole months. Barbara Petrovna inspected her estates, consulted her managers, and attended the sale of the corn which had been collected in barns, and immense corn stacks were so arranged that the carriage with its four horses abreast could easily pass between them. I must explain that the corn had been brought from several estates to be sold in one place.

On one of these journeys we arrived at Sychevo, which

now, it appears, belongs to Nicholas Sergeyevich's wife's niece, Madame Malyarevska. This village was between sixteen and seventeen miles from Spasskoye; from it, sturgeon and trout were often sent alive to Spasskoye from the Sychevo pond, where they were plentiful.

Arriving in this village, Barbara Petrovna and the rest of us were struck by the unusual size of one of the peasants ploughing in the field.

Barbara Petrovna ordered the carriage to be stopped, and the giant sent for.

For a long time they called him from a distance, and at last, as they approached him, he replied to all the words and signs made by a kind of roar.

It seemed that he had been deaf and dumb from birth.

The bailiff was sent for, and he explained that dumb Andrew was sober, industrious, and an unusually well-behaved peasant in spite of his lifelong defect.

But I think that, in addition to Andrew's stature and comeliness, this defect increased still more his originality and captivated Barbara Petrovna. She there and then decided to take the dumb man into her service, as one of her personal servants, and she appointed him handyman. From that day he was called the " dumb."

How this was done, or whether Andrew was willing to change his work as a peasant for the easier work in his mistress's house, I do not know. Had I been older at the time I should probably not have noticed it. It was common enough in those days ; suddenly, for no reason whatever, the landowner would take it into his head to turn a peasant into a domestic serf, or make him a shoe-maker, a joiner, or tailor, or cook. Sometimes it was considered a special favour, but no-one ever took the trouble to find out whether he or his family wanted such a change.

At that time, with all my love and pity for the serfs,

I yet never thought of being sorry for Andrew, who had been torn so suddenly from his own soil and his own fields, and it was only after having read *Mumu* that I made inquiries of eye-witnesses, and found that, at first, he had really been very unhappy.

Ah! One must have that love and sympathy for the serfs which our never-to-be-forgotten Ivan Sergeyevich had, in order to enter into the feelings and innermost world of our people.

He, however, knew that the "dumb" had suffered and wept, and none of us had paid any attention.

But it is a consolation to know that Andrew was probably not very long unhappy, because, until that unfortunate affair of Mumu, he was generally rather jolly, and was very devoted to his mistress, who, for her part, was kindly disposed towards him.

Barbara Petrovna was very proud of her giant *dvornik* (handyman). He was always very neatly dressed, and would not wear or wish to wear any but red cotton shirts: in winter he wore a fine sheepskin jacket, and in summer, a cotton sleeveless undercoat, or blue peasant's jacket.

In Moscow the bright green barrel, and the handsome dapple grey horse from our own stud, with which Andrew went for water, were very popular at the fountain near the Alexandrine garden. There everybody acknowledged the Turgenev dumb handyman, greeted him in friendly fashion, and talked to him by signs.

Andrew's face, noticeably huge, but perfectly proportioned to his gigantic stature, always shone with a good-natured smile. His strength was extraordinary, and his hands were so big that, when he happened to take me in his arms, I felt as if I were in some sort of carriage; and it was in this manner that he once took me to his room, where I saw Mumu for the first time.

A tiny little dog, white with brown spots, lay on Andrew's bed. From that day onwards, more and more was I scolded by Agashenka for the crumbs of white bread and pieces of sugar that she shook out of my pocket. They were the remains of dainties that I gave on the quiet to Andrew for Mumu. We were both very fond of that little dog!

Everybody knows the unhappy fate of Mumu, with this difference only, that the devotion of Andrew to his mistress remained unchanged. However bitterly he felt his loss, he remained faithful to his mistress, and served her until her death. And he never wished to acknowledge anyone else as his master.

But before we quite take leave of our " Gerasim," so well known to all of us, I will relate a rather amusing anecdote about him.

In 1850, on Easter Day, someone who was not in Barbara Petrovna's good graces, decided to give the dumb handyman some blue-printed calico for a shirt.

Whether Andrew shared his mistress's dislike for this person, or whether he preferred to wear only red shirts, I do not know, but he looked scornfully at the calico, uttered his one and only sound, ugh ! and threw the calico on the bench.

At that time Barbara Petrovna's health was already very bad, and she had with her constantly as nurse and housekeeper, Alexandra Mikhaylovna Medvyedeva, a well-born widow.

One of her duties in the evening, before going to bed, was to rub Barbara Petrovna's legs. The swelling and pain arising from the dropsy that was coming on, and from which Barbara Petrovna died, prevented her from sleeping.

This evening Mme. Medvyedeva, knowing, of course, that such a thing would please her mistress, did not fail to relate Andrew's adventure with the printed calico.

Barbara Petrovna's voice actually shook with pleasure. " Did he really do that ? " she asked.

Mme. Medvyedeva told her about it, and that Andrew had pointed to his red shirt, and explained by a sign, that his mistress gave him many like it.

At nine o'clock next morning the bell rang ; the mistress was awakĕ and the shutters were opened.

The chief maid went in, put the toilet articles as usual on the bed, and brought up a little table and a cup of tea.

" Call the ' dumb ' " said Barbara Petrovna.

The maid was startled.

" I said, call Andrew. Don't you hear ? "

The chambermaid went out, perplexed ; however, she decided to call.

At first our giant was taken into the maids' room.

Then they reported : " Andrew is here."

" Tell him to come here, to my bedroom ; only wash him ! "

There, in the maids' room, the " dumb " underwent such a scouring as he had never before had in his life.

The girls, of whom there were probably ten, each one with difficulty suppressing her laughter, endeavoured to lend a hand at putting a resplendent polish on Andrew.

At last they had washed him, brushed him, and even annointed his head with my pomade.

They explained to him by signs that he had to appear before his mistress.

While his toilet was in progress, Andrew groaned enough to be heard nearly all over the house, but smiled joyfully.

Barbara Petrovna called me and ordered me to give her a blue ribbon. The butler was also sent for.

" A nice red one ! " said Barbara Petrovna. As she was still not accustomed to counting in silver, that meant a ten-rouble note (three silver roubles).

The red note was brought. And at last Andrew was led solemnly in. All the glasses, bottles and cups on Barbara Petrovna's bed and dressing table shook and trembled under the weight of Andrew's steps.

He roared and laughed in a deafening manner with pleasure and joy; but when the chief maid, who was bringing him into his mistress's apartments, waved her hands at him to check him, he shook his head all the more violently, and at last fell into the room, first lowering his head to avoid striking it on the lintel of the door.

Barbara Petrovna smiled good naturedly; with one hand she pointed to the blue ribbon to indicate the despised present, and she stretched out her other hand with the red note in it.

The chambermaid who was standing there, made a sign to him that he must kiss his mistress's hand, which he did, awkwardly enough, as such an honour did not often come his way.

On going out, he pointed to his mistress with his finger and thumped himself on the chest, which meant in his language, that he loved her very much. He even forgave her for Mumu's death.

But it was noticed that after the tragic death of his little favourite, he never fondled another dog. And that is how it happened that our journey to Sychevo, later on gave Ivan Sergeyevich material for a charming story.

*   *   *   *

It so happened that on one of our journeys into the country, we arrived at Kholodovo.

Barbara Petrovna had no pleasant recollections of this place. There she had spent her miserable childhood in her stepfather's house.

The old, uninhabited squire's house was almost in ruins; in some places even the windows were broken.

Having rested a little while after her journey, Barbara Petrovna went through all the rooms . . . I, of course with her.

We entered a narrow, long and rather dark hall. Everywhere the family portraits on the walls looked at us from their blackened gilt frames in a very unfriendly manner. On a step at the bottom of the hall stood a white column on which was a bust of Peter Ivanovich Lutovinov, Barbara Petrovna's father. Among the portraits, for some reason or other, was placed a head by Greuze[1]: the girl with the dove.

From the hall we went into a corridor or adjoining room, and I was struck by a door boarded up with planks laid crosswise.

But I had scarcely got up to it, and touched with my hand the old fashioned copper lock sticking out of the boards, when Barbara Petrovna seized me by the hand:—

"Don't touch it! You mustn't! These rooms are accursed!"

Never shall I forget her voice and face. So much fear, hatred and malice did they express! I hadn't recovered when she dragged me quickly, quickly further away.

Her fear communicated itself to me. What was it that I imagined? I don't know, but I was glad to run away from something, and kept looking round to see if anything was following us.

[1] 1726-1805. Jean Batiste.

Afterwards I learned that the boarded up door led into the room formerly occupied by her stepfather, at whose hands she had suffered so much.

There, at Kholodovo I saw the armchair in which Ivan Sergeyevich's grandmother died, having first paid the priest for the prayers for the dying.

Casting my mind back over my life and conduct at Barbara Petrovna's, thereby remembering her love for me, and all that she was to me, I should again like to say a few words in her defence. Some of her actions did arouse indignation; I myself, not having escaped from her extremely oppressive authority, often criticized her, and found myself on the point of opposing her. But she herself was at variance with life. And who would not have been embittered by such persecution and misery?

Her childhood and youth were horrible; her marriage did not bring her what every woman expects from it—love. In her own mind she knew that her handsome husband loved, not her, but her possessions, and that she was for him a good, advantageous match. Sergius Nikolayevich was often unfaithful to his wife, and she knew it.

Her children—I do not blame them—did not fulfil her ambition or justify her hopes.

The elder married against her will. The younger became a "writer," which in her eyes was equal to earning money in some kind of trade. What was left to her for her own intimate, personal life? Only wealth, and the power to rule over her serfs!

She did not see her son's fame. *Khor and Kalinich*[1] could hardly have aroused her enthusiasm. She didn't even read it.

It was in 1845 that Ivan Sergeyevich began to write,

[1] See translation and detailed reference to it in Sir John Maynard's Essays.

and he spoke to his mother of his intention to go abroad again. She was very much dissatisfied, and tried hard to dissuade him.

He spent the whole of that year at Spasskoye, and every family and annual festival was marked by some happening that testified to Barbara Petrovna's wretched frame of mind.

Ivan Sergeyevich's desire to go abroad, news about Nicholas and the journey to see him, quarrels with her brother-in-law, all had a very bad influence on Barbara Petrovna. She revenged herself for all these misfortunes and disappointments on those who surrounded her.

Chapter Nine

BARBARA PETROVNA FEIGNS DEATH

In that same year 1845 a fresh sorrow befell Barbara Petrovna. At the end of the winter she had almost finally broken with her brother-in-law, Nicholas Nikolayevich Turgenev, who until that time had been a bachelor in charge of all her estates. In 1846 he married, consequently he found interests of his own in life, which was something that Barbara Petrovna would never tolerate in those closely connected with her. She kept around her only those who looked upon her as the centre of all their thoughts.

They separated and, in spite of repeated attempts on her brother-in-law's part, she remained inexorable.

I cannot avoid devoting a few lines to the memory of this sincerely good and excellent man. Everybody who knew him, loved him. We all called him uncle, and he was the uncle who spoiled us all. As regards the people under him, minor agents, clerks, bailiffs and all the servants, everybody worshipped him, no-one was afraid of him, and he did evil to none. On the contrary, he was the defender of all those who were at fault, and he carefully concealed anything that could arouse Barbara Petrovna's anger. There were times when Barbara Petrovna ordered someone to be exiled; seeing that such a cruel punishment was undeserved, and was only the result of Barbara Petrovna's whim, he banished the culprit to another estate; the exile was out of sight, but at the same time his well-being was still cared for.

In such a manner, many unfortunate people were saved from an unhappy fate, and this was always kept secret from Barbara Petrovna.

Ivan Sergeyevich was his uncle's idol. He loved no-one as much as he did this nephew.

I wept bitterly at Nicholas Nikolayevich's departure, and was not scolded for it. I was even allowed to correspond with him. In answer I received the most affectionate letters from him, full of assurances that his new life and ties would never efface from his heart his feelings of love and esteem for Barbara Petrovna, and that she had only to say one word, and he would again be to her what he had formerly been, that is, her most devoted friend and brother.

But Barbara Petrovna would never allow me even to read his letters to her, and later on they were all taken away suddenly from me, and a continuation of the correspondence was forbidden. I have kept only two of his letters: one dated August 16th, the year not stated, and the other April, 1850.

All this affair, the search for new estate agents, business of the estate and other things—all this had a very bad effect on Barbara Petrovna's character, and certainly on her stubborn temper.

Everything went wrong that year. I sat oftener as a punishment in the winter garden adjoining her study; sometimes I was shut up there the whole day, but I must own that this imprisonment did not trouble me very much that year. It was better to sit alone among the flowers with the greenfinches, goldfinches and tomtits flying about freely in my prison, than to be under mamma's eyes; for then our excellent butler Vassily Ivanovich never forgot to bring me a double portion of the sweet when mamma was having her afternoon sleep.

It was terribly hard to be in Barbara Petrovna's presence. If I sat at my lessons, she would question me; my governess would tremble, and I would be so terrified that everything flew out of my head at the very sight of her frowning face.

If I sat at work in the drawing-room:—" How are you holding your needle? . . . Why are you always silent?"

If I began to talk . . . "Why are you always chattering?"

If I let the scissors fall: " *Maladroite!*" and the fall of the little scissors gave her such a fright, that she had to have smelling salts to help to soothe her nerves, and then my troubles began.

"You know that I am upset and ill, and that the least noise affects my nerves. You're ungrateful! You don't think of anything! No, it isn't thoughtlessness . . . no, you do it on purpose! You want to kill me by your conduct, you do everything on purpose!"

After such a rebuke, it was, of course, impossible to be cheerful. I really loved Barbara Petrovna, and such a cutting rebuke was particularly painful when I was ready to do anything to please her.

It would have been difficult for an adult to hide her grief, how much more so for a child! I was miserable.

A harsh exclamation: "Come here!"

I did. "What's the matter with you? I'm asking you. Well?"

I made no reply.

"What's the matter with you? Are you ill?"

"No, mamma. I am well."

"Ah! ha! Now I understand," answered Barbara Petrovna. "You are sulking! That's the last straw!"

And again a whole torrent of reproaches, and banishment either to the hall or to my tomtits.

The next day, again a rebuke for something or other.

Then I tried to be cheerful to show that I was not annoyed; once again that wasn't right. . . .

"What's pleasing you? It's all the same to you whether

I blame or praise you. You are an unfeeling, ungrateful creature!" and the tone of her voice was raised. "What! I scold you and you just chatter and laugh! Away with you!"

And so it went on, a continual nagging. "You don't know how to hold yourself, or how to talk!"

Driven from her sight, I breathed more freely, but not for long. One of the servants would be sent for. More trouble!

She was terribly fond of embarrassing people, and for a long time she would plague the servant who had been sent for with questions: "What is this? What does it mean?"

The unfortunate servant would stand for a long time hesitating, not even knowing why his mistress was angry with him.

Thus it happened that Barbara Petrovna was standing near one of the windows in the flower-filled drawing room. and she called for the gardener. To her question: "What is this? What does it mean?" he was silent.

"Why don't you answer? What is it?"

"I don't know."

"Be quiet! Who should know if you don't?"

The unfortunate servant's perplexity continued.

"Have you watered the flowers to-day?"

"Yes, I have."

"You lie! What's this?" At this she pointed to one of the bowls of flowers. "You haven't watered this."

It would be wrong whether he answered or not.

"You didn't water them all!"

"Yes, madame, I did. I watered them all."

"Be quiet! How dare you be rude! You will all worry me into my grave. You have forgotten that I can banish you! I will exile you all! Call Polyakov."

Andrew Ivanovich appeared; his unhappy wife stood near the door and trembled for her husband.

Again the same question: " What is it," etc.? Gratified at Polyakov's perplexity, Barbara Petrovna continued: —

"What sort of a steward are you? What kind of a servant have I got if you can't prevent the others from being rude to me! You will all find yourselves banished! All of you, I'll banish you all!"

And the same thing every day.

October 28th of this year remains to this day in the memory of all those who are still living. Fathers and mothers tell this story to their children; and when we meet we always mention Barbara Petrovna's extraordinary prank.

Her sons' birthdays and name days, and mine, were always celebrated in a festive manner, even if the person in question was absent.

So this 28th of October, Ivan Sergeyevich's birthday had to be celebrated in accordance with the usual established order.

This order has often been described in numerous chronicles relating to landowning families.

It was the same thing everywhere and always; there was a long table laid, with pies, roast geese, pork, or, on fast days, fish ; everything was cut up into portions, and at one end of the table were decanters of effervescent wine (the name given to vodka in the province of Orel).

On the women's half were *hors d'œuvre*, a samovar, and red home-made wine for the fair sex.

In 1882 I congratulated Ivan Sergeyevich on his birthday for the last time, and reminded him of the festival on that day in his mother's house.

At Spasskoye the table for the men was laid in the library, that is, in our worthy Michael Philipovich's living room. On such days the old man was specially miserable; so much of his mistress's food was going to be eaten!

At the entrance to the long gallery was an armchair for Barbara Petrovna. Each of the servants, according to rank and dignity, kissed hands, then went to the wine, and having taken a glass, bowed to his mistress a second time, and drank his allowance.

Michael Philipovich was the first, then Polyakov.

The ceremony passed off this time much as usual, but Barbara Petrovna looked rather gloomy, and there was a feeling that something unpleasant might happen. However the day and the dinner ended happily; it even appeared that she was beginning to be more cheerful.

That day was the name day of the principal "keeper of the linen" Praskovia Mikhaylovna.

I must say, in passing, that Barbara Petrovna, with all her despotism, looked after her servants very well, and fed them excellently; bachelors and spinsters dined together, and families received a plentiful allowance monthly: flour, groats, butter, fats, meat and fish. They could keep cows and poultry at their mistress's expense, they received an allowance of tea, and a wage in money as well.

It was understood that the servants were allowed a certain amount of money for festivals, and as the linen keeper was one of the aristocrats among them, her name day was celebrated.

Barbara Petrovna knew that she was giving a party that evening. This is what happened; suddenly, about nine o'clock in the evening, a terrible rumour spread through the house:—

"The mistress is ill! The mistress is dying! Send for the priest!"

The first time I read Bossuet's celebrated funeral oration on the death of the English Queen Henrietta: *"Oh! nuit*

desastreus! Madame se meurt, Madame est morte!" I
immediately remembered, and remember now, our remarkable 28th of October, 1845, when the rumour which caused
so much consternation went all round Spasskoye:—

" The mistress is dying! "

They sent for the priest; Barbara Petrovna herself, in a
very weak voice, asked for him. She made her confession
and when the priest proposed to administer the last sacrament, she explained that she wanted to bless me first, and
say good-bye to everyone.

In the same faint voice she ordered Agatha to bring Ivan
Sergeyevich's portrait (a copy of which appeared in "European News," 1884), also Nicholas's portrait.

" *Adieu, Jean! Adieu, Nicholas! Adieu, mes enfants!"*
repeated Barbara Petrovna.

I was on my knees near her bed, and wept so bitterly
and so loudly that our good Porphyry Timofeyevich
forced me to swallow a few drops of water to soothe me.

But when Barbara Petrovna ordered them to bring the
icon of the Holy Virgin of Vladimir[1], and blessed me, my
sobs became a hysterical shriek; they took me out of the
room to quieten me a little.

Porphyry Timofeyevich continued to stand calmly at his
mistress's bed, with his never failing drops. Agatha stood
at the head of the bed, and fanned her mistress with a
cloth dipped in vinegar.

Barbara Petrovna demanded that all her household servants, forty in number, and all her office staff, numbering
about ten, beginning with the chief clerk, and the cashier
having charge of her affairs, and the rest should come and
say good-bye to her, because she felt that she was dying.

When this was done, and they were all assembled, she

[1] This icon is now mine, and has that date and year marked on the
reverse side.

ordered them to come one by one and take leave of her.

She lay with half closed eyes, and with her left hand hanging down.

Each one of the servants came in, bowed to the ground before his mistress, and having kissed her hand, withdrew, making way for the next.

When the last one's turn came she asked: "Is that all?"

"Yes, madame," answered Polyakov, who, as chief steward, was also standing near the bed, supervising the ceremony of hand kissing.

"Ah! Ah!" repeated Barbara Petrovna.

I kept on crying.

"Stop crying," said Barbara Petrovna caressingly, and she put her hand on my head, "Stop crying, God is merciful, perhaps I shall not die. I am feeling better."

"Agatha! Some tea!"

Of course, I, as a child, was convinced that I was going to lose my dear benefactress, and for a long time I could not restrain my tears; but the doctor, Agatha and her husband knew that all this was nothing but a farce, and were only doubtful as to what would come of it. They had not to wait long for an explanation! Barbara Petrovna drank two cups of tea; the priest who was awaiting his summons in the hall, was sent away, and she became calm.

So about an hour went by.

"Polyakov!" exclaimed Barbara Petrovna's stentorian voice, terrifying everybody because it signified that something extraordinary was coming.

"Bring some paper! Write!"

On a little table near the bed was a box in the form of a book, on which was written, in French of course, "Loose leaves." In this box there were sheets of paper, on which she either wrote herself, or ordered others to write her plans, intentions, etc., for reference.

Polyakov took some paper, and in pencil began to write the following, dictated by his mistress:—

"*To-morrow morning, these culprits must appear in front of my windows, and sweep the yard and garden: Nicholas Yakovlev, Ivan Petrov, Yegora Kondratyev,*" and so on. She recited the names of all those who had been absent from her leave taking, and of all those who, she noticed, had been under the influence of drink at that time.

When all the names were written down, she merely announced:—

"Carry this out," and she signed the order in her own hand.

"Rascals, drunkards! You were all drunk. You were glad that your mistress was dying!" She spoke in jerks.

She quite forgot that they had all drunk a good deal before they heard the sad news of her pretended approaching death.

"You were overjoyed that I was dying! You were drinking and celebrating a name day, and your mistress dying!"

This went on for a long time in the same tone.

This time, I remember, I had no very great sympathy for the culprits. I was very fond of Barbara Petrovna, and my joy at seeing that she was better prevented me from pitying those who were doomed to sweep the yard.

The following day, all the culprits, not even excluding the principal servants in the house and office, in grey smocks, with circles and crosses chalked on their backs, appeared with shovels and brooms, in front of their mistress's windows, and vigorously cleaned out the yard and flower garden.

Chapter Ten

TURGENEV DISCUSSES SERFDOM

It was during that same year that all of us at Spasskoye and all visitors there had no Easter week celebrations. We all know that Easter is considered the greatest festival of rejoicing and triumph. We all know how everyone awaits the cheerful chime of the bells, after the mournful, long drawn out Lenten tolling. And the children? Who, remembering his childhood's years, does not think of how he waited for his sweet, tasty Easter cake, and with what impatience he wanted to see and eat the first red egg. During my childhood it happened that I had no Easter cake, no sweets, not even the festival itself.

But before I explain how it happened, I must mention one thing that could not be repeated to-day, thanks to the introduction of schools in many of the villages.

Children of all classes to-day know the prayers and the church service, even something of what a festival means, and they know nearly everything that is sung in church on special days. It was not so at that time. In squires' families, of which Barbara Petrovna's was one, there were always young girls to run errands, as it was termed. With us, their duty was to sit constantly in their mistress's dressing-room, and be ready to appear at the first call. They were in twos and threes. One of them, my Agatha's sister, was my first and best friend. Although I wasn't even supposed to speak to her, we always found means of chatting and playing, and we shared each other's childish joys and sorrows. My favourite's name was Liza. She knew how to read, but she neither knew nor understood the prayers and the church service.

I knew just a little more. The parts of the service that I knew were the Liturgy, Vespers, and the Te Deum.

I was not allowed to go to matins on the solemn days in Holy week and Easter week, but from Liza and others I learned that there was a specially fine service from Good Friday to Saturday.

I was very devout, and my greatest desire was to attend church that day. But my timid request was answered so sternly that I dared not persist, but my longing to go to church was all the greater.

At first, in our consultations, I persuaded Liza to wait for me in the porch; I determined not to go to sleep before matins, and as soon as I heard the first sound of the bell, to get up and, if mamma still slept, to go out quietly, dress myself, and run to church. But on further consideration, this plan could not be carried out, and we decided not to make any attempt to escape. Liza was to go alone, and I begged her to listen attentively, and watch every detail, so that she could tell me about it afterwards.

The next day, that is Saturday, I awaited with feverish impatience the moment when I should see her.

"Well, what was it like? Tell me every little thing," I urged her.

"Ah! young lady, how wonderful it was! Jesus Christ was buried, that is, His image was buried."

"How buried?" I was doubtful.

"Yes, they buried Him. They took Him straight from the church to the cemetery."

"Well, and what then?"

"They have left Him in the chapel there until Sunday." I believed her. "And what did they sing?"

"What did they sing? They sang beautifully! All sang, the clerks and all the choir, they sang so well and so slowly."

"And what words did they sing?" I wanted to know everything.

"Words? Of course these: 'May our Lord Jesus Christ rest with the saints!'"

I believed this too, and only regretted all the more that I had not been present at such a solemn service.

Easter Sunday came. The mass was early, and the bells began to chime at seven or eight o'clock. First came the sexton himself, and I must own that he was a real master of his work. Neither before nor since, in any village church have I heard such a skilful chime. So he began, and down below the boys were impatiently waiting their turn to ring for the great festival.

I awoke, and with joy and emotion, listened to the peal of the bells, which, in my imagination, meant something special; I even ran to the window to look through the shutters at this great day. What kind of a day was it?

"Where are you going?" Barbara Petrovna called out.

My acute, practised ear heard a storm coming. I hastily dived into bed, and even pulled the blanket over my head.

Mamma rang. Agatha went in.

"What's that noise?" asked her mistress.

From precaution, and in order to fathom the meaning of the question, Agatha was silent.

"I asked you what that noise is?"

" It is the festival, Madame, Easter," was the timid reply.

"Easter! Festival! What festival? I ought to have been asked what I intended to do at Easter. I am ill, suffering. The bells disturb me. They must be stopped immediately," finished Barbara Petrovna angrily.

"There is no Easter week for me," she continued, "and there must not be one for anyone living with me here. Tell the priest that I am ill, and that I cannot do with the noise of the bells."

And they were all ringing more and more joyfully, and I was listening with such eagerness. Then they began to die down, and I wanted to keep on listening until the order had been carried out. Then all was quiet. More than an hour passed in dead silence.

At nine o'clock Barbara Petrovna ordered me to get up and dress. I went out and put on my fine, embroidered white dress.

I had to wait until mamma's shutters were opened, and her tea had been taken in; after this I had to go in and read my chapter of the *Imitation of Jesus Christ*.

But the shutters were not opened, the mistress was ill, her tea was taken to her and I went in.

I stopped in perplexity. Ought I to give her an Easter kiss, or simply say: *bonjour, maman?*

She held out her hand and kissed me as usual on the forehead.

"What are you dressed up for?" she asked in a weak voice. "You will dirty yourself. Change your dress and go away and drink your tea."

And in the hall the table was laid for a state occasion! The Sèvres porcelain service, that was used only on very special occasions, was on a tray. The samovar had a special festival brilliance, and the butler, Vassily Ivanovich, in a tail coat and white gloves, stood ready to pour out tea. The Paschal dish was so fragrant, the eggs so bright red, and the lamb made of butter lay so meekly on a little plate, with a green branch in its mouth! The Easter cake even drowned the scent of vanilla in the neighbouring dish, which had been so well prepared by our cook, Saveliy Matveyevich. Everything, it seemed, spoke of a festival, and behold, we were not to have one!

I parted from my pretty little dress indifferently enough, and hastened to put on another one, so that I

could go as quickly as possible into the hall. But alas!
What a great disappointment awaited me!

There, the council had gathered, consisting of Andrew
Ivanovich, chief steward, his wife Agatha, my English
Miss Blackwood, my Russian teacher Michael Alexye-
vich Potarov, the butler Vassily Ivanovich, and the housekeeper Praskovia Ivanovna. The great question to be
decided was: were they to break their fast, or simply drink
tea?

"What did the mistress say to you?" asked the steward
of his wife.

"What? I've told you a hundred times," answered his
wife sadly. "She said there was to be no festival, that was
all."

"Did she say anything about the Paschal dish?" questioned the butler.

"No, she didn't say anything about that," replied
Agatha.

"Well then!" Polyakov was overjoyed. His kindheartedness wanted his mistress's silence about the Paschal dish
to mean that it could be eaten.

"Well then, what about it!" interrupted his wife
harshly. She was much quicker and cleverer than her
husband.

"Well then, perhaps it does mean that."

"Be quiet! You'll only get into trouble."

Suddenly they all turned to me, as if they expected me
to decide this important question.

"Did mamma say anything to you, young lady?"

"She ordered me to change my dress and go. . . ."

" But what did she say?" interrupted Agatha. "Did she
mention the Paschal dish? "

"No——" I answered truly but very hesitatingly.

"Well then!" Again our excellent Polyakov was triumphant.

"Oh! Be quiet, please!" snapped his wife. "I should say, clear all this away. It would be wiser to put an end to all this doubt. Vassya, take it away!"

"Perhaps we shall be able to break our fast at lunch," my dear Andrew Ivanovich did not fail to comfort me in a whisper. "How can you expect such a thing!" Agatha, knowing her mistress's character better than any of us, destroyed my hopes pitilessly.

And in two minutes all these festival preparations were cleared away from the table, and we sat there, drinking tea, just as on a weekday and an ordinary day.

To console me, I had a cake, but not one that had been blessed in Church.

I must own that I swallowed tears, not tea. God forbid that I should begin to cry! Mamma might call me, and would see my red eyes. That would mean trouble.

We got up from the table. Miss Blackwood took her Bible. Michael Philipovich went into his wing, and I was alone.

Breakfast and dinner went by. We walked about noiselessly, and spoke in whispers. Barbara Petrovna's shutters were not opened. She did not leave her bedroom, she breakfasted and dined alone. The priests came with the cross, they were not received; the mistress was ill. When would she be better? Couldn't say! I did not even hear the "Christ is risen."

In consequence of suppressing my tears for the whole day, I had a sore throat. Not understanding then the cause of this pain, I spoke about it to my governess, and, to crown all, they rubbed a stocking with soap and lard and tied it round my neck.

But all the same, I did eat of the Paschal dish. It was Liza, my secret little friend, who proved to be my benefactress.

In her pocket, in paper, she brought me a little piece of the Easter dish, without sugar, without vanilla, and even the curds not quite fresh; I ate it with great devotion, first crossing myself.

So passed Easter day in complete silence. On Wednesday or Thursday, on entering her mistress's bedroom, Agatha heard for the first time the word . . . " Shutters !"

But before breakfast, to the butler's question "Will you, madame, break your fast with the Easter dish?" Barbara Petrovna replied: "What's the good now? The festival is nearly over, and, after all, everything is probably spoiled."

And so that year we had no Easter celebrations, and the bells were not rung.

In 1846 Ivan Sergeyevich went abroad, having received a rather modest sum of money from his mother.

He was particularly melancholy during the last days before his departure, and in my memory during all the years that followed, I never see him other than thoughtful and unhappy, quite different from what my childish imagination had pictured him.

I inadvertently happened to take part in one of his last conversations with his mother and I received a stern rebuke for my ill-timed interference.

"I don't know what you are talking about," I heard Barbara Petrovna's voice as I went into the adjoining room. What had been said before my appearance I do not know. "So my people are badly treated! What more do they need? They are very well fed, shod, and clothed, they are even paid wages. Just tell me how many serfs do receive wages!"

" I did not say that they starve or are not well clothed," began Ivan Sergeyevich cautiously, stammering a little, "but see how they all tremble before you!"

"Well, and what of it!" interrupted his mother, in a voice that clearly meant, and so they ought!

"But mamma, just think what it must be like for a man to live constantly in such a state of fear! Imagine a whole life of fear, and nothing but fear! Their grandfathers, their fathers, and they themselves are all afraid . . . must their children also be doomed?"

"What fear? What are you talking about?" Barbara Petrovna was annoyed.

"The fear of not being safe for a day, or for a single hour of their existence; to-day here, to-morrow there, where you will. That is not life!"

"I don't understand you."

"Listen, mamma, couldn't you now, this minute "— Ivan Sergeyevich was becoming more and more excited —"if you wanted, couldn't you exile any one of them?"

"Of course I could."

"And if I ask you why?"

"If they deserve it."

"And if they don't? Couldn't you still do it, from a whim alone?"

"Of course I could."

"Then that only proves what I have always told you. . . . They are not people . . . they are things!"

"Then, according to you, they ought to be freed?"

"No, why? I don't say that, the time hasn't yet come."

"And won't come!" said Barbara Petrovna decidedly.

"Yes, it will come, and it will come soon," cried Ivan Sergeyevich passionately, and in the rather shrill voice he used when excited, and he walked quickly round the room.

"Sit down, your walking about worries me," his mother reproved him.

"And so my people are badly treated . . ." she continued,

she was insulted. "Who told you? And is it really possible to get on without fear—"

"Yes, much is possible, all is possible! Can it really be that you, with your keen knowledge of people, do not see in them any love, or devotion, or a feeling. . . ."

"What's the matter with you, Jean? Have you gone mad? From whom have you heard that I. . . ."

My heart sank within me, I gasped.

The evening before, I had told Ivan Sergeyevich a good deal about the sufferings of Agatha and her husband, and just then the thought flashed into my mind that he might speak about them.

It is impossible to explain how quickly all this came into my mind, and how quickly I decided to act; I picked up the first book I could lay hands on—I see now that it was *Granvile's Caricatures*—and determined to interrupt this conversation, and then to make a sign to Ivan Sergeyevich.

"Mamma, may I take this book?" . . . I rushed impetuously into the room, feeling that I was as pale as death.

"What do you want?" cried mamma. "What do you mean by interrupting? You were listening, we were talking business! Go away!"

I had got to the door, when suddenly I heard behind me:—

"Come back! What's the matter with you? Your face. . . ."

"With me? Nothing."

"What do you mean, nothing? You are lying. You are whiter than my handkerchief. Are you ill?"

"Yes, my head aches."

"If your head aches you don't need a book! Put it down and go!" I went out, and stood near the door, trying to attract Ivan Sergeyevich's attention.

But he was bent down, his head resting in his hands, and he could not see me. All my caution was in vain Our dear Ivan Sergeyevich himself suddenly discovered and understood that the thing had gone too far: because, when his mother, wishing to continue the conversation, asked : —

"Tell me, now, what have you heard?"
he replied: "Of course I have heard nothing. I only wanted to express my own opinion. I find that generally the men serfs are not men, but things that can be moved about, ruined, destroyed . . . a terrible state really!"

"And what of it?" inquired Barbara Petrovna.

"How can I tell you . . . no, let us leave it, really you . . ." and again he walked quickly about the room.

"Why are you saying all this?" His mother obstinately wanted to continue.

"Well . . ." and becoming silent for a while, he stopped in front of his mother. "I wanted to talk to you about my brother, mamma. Why are you angry with him? You know how short of money he is."

"That is the last straw!" Barbara Petrovna flared up. "It all depends on him, and you know it."

"But he can't abandon . . ." Ivan was beginning. . . .

"Are you bidding me consent to his marriage?"

"And why not?"

"I see that you are quite mad!" . . . and Barbara Petrovna poured a whole torrent of reproaches and complaints on her elder son, then turned on her younger son. She ransacked her memory, and complained of everything.

Ivan Sergeyevich had been imprudent enough to tell his mother suddenly that one of his works had been criticized. Either Barbara Petrovna misunderstood the real meaning of criticism, or she just wanted to quarrel with the word in order to attack her son; but the affair ended with the doctor and his drops.

"You, a squire, a Turgenev!" she shouted, "and you let any son of a priest criticize you!"

"But mamma, if they criticize, it means that they have taken some notice of it, and I am glad! I am not a nobody if I am talked about."

"And how do they talk about you? How do they discuss you? They blame you, they call you a fool, and you bow down to them . . . eh? What's the good of your education, all the tutors and professors I provided for you? One of you throws me over for a woman very much beneath him, and you, my Benjamin, are wasted as an author. . . ."

Then followed tears, sobs and hysterics. . . .

The doctor appeared with his drops. Ivan Sergeyevich was alarmed. He began to kiss his mother's hands, and he did all he could to calm her.

"Oh, do stop, mamma! Calm yourself! Forgive me; this conversation hasn't given me any pleasure. . . ."

"How can I be calm, how can I help being distressed . . ." continued Barbara Petrovna with real tears ". . . when you have decided to go abroad again?"

And then again began reproaches, and an enumeration of all the advantages of service, marriage, and life in Russia near her.

Those were Ivan Sergeyevich's most difficult moments, for what could he reply to all his mother's complaints?

He bowed his head in his hands, and was silent, then, with a griefstricken, almost despairing expression, he turned away.

And he, and all of us quite understood that Barbara Petrovna's temporary kindness and indulgence were maintained only during her rare and short meetings with her son.

He stayed with her, but she could not keep him long, as he was only a silent and impotent witness of things he could not endure, and yet had not the power to help. This could not be easy for anyone, so he went away!

Chapter Eleven

BARBARA PETROVNA'S RELATIONS WITH HER ENTOURAGE

In November, 1846, I entered Mme. Knol's boarding school, where, by a strange caprice of Barbara Petrovna, instead of my own name Bogdanovich, I used the name Lutovinov, and by that name, until I married, I was known to my friends. The certificates given to me, and signed by the professors and lecturers in the school, were also given in the name of the student Barbara Lutovinov.

In June, 1847, we went to Spasskoye, and there, without a break, Barbara Petrovna stayed until September, 1849, but I was sent, during term time, to Moscow to school.

From this time on, in many of my stories I shall be obliged to talk about myself. I had already left childhood behind, and had ceased to be just a passive looker-on; often and often it fell to my lot to play a real and painful part; and sometimes it happened that I was either a secret or open mediator between Barbara Petrovna and her sons.

I lived at the school with my governess Sophya Danilovna Ivanovna, chosen for me by Barbara Petrovna. Her duty was to accompany me to church for festivals, and to drive daily with me in a splendid carriage, drawn either by a pair or four magnificent horses. I had special privileges at Mme. Knol's. I had my own room, my servants, a very handsome Meybohm piano, a special music teacher, the then well-known G——, and so on.

I should not mention all these things relating to me personally if the same advantages had been enjoyed by Barbara Petrovna's sons. While she was spending so much money on my education, and on luxury that I could have done very well without, she would not send even a cent to her own children, and her generosity to me weighed more and more heavily on my conscience.

Barbara Petrovna's displeasure with her sons grew even stronger. It may be that sometimes separation from them grieved her, if we believe what she wrote in a letter to me on November 18th, 1847 : —

"*I have never been so anxious, I am very much worried about you. When shall I have my family with me? When shall I see you all, my children? I do not even see one of the three of you.*"

At that time she was very anxious to find a head agent for all her estates. She did not want to be reconciled to her brother-in-law, Nicholas Nikolayevich Turgenev, and in one of her letters to me she even demanded that I should no longer look upon him as someone near and dear to me.

Quite by chance, and unexpectedly, Barbara Petrovna found a man to whom she could entrust her affairs. At that time Ivan Mikhaylovich Bakunin lived at Mtsensk. He came quite often to see us; the conversation turned on housekeeping, and the difficulties of administering estates that were situated in different provinces and districts ; the affair ended in Barbara Petrovna's asking Bakunin to undertake the work of being supreme ruler of her five thousand serfs, just as her brother-in-law had been.

Knowing Barbara Petrovna's disposition, Bakunin would not consent for a long time, and when he did consent, to tell the truth he was not on very good terms with his principal. He was well educated and a man of the world, and, consequently, he would not submit slavishly to Barbara Petrovna, nor would he manœuvre or hide anything.

He was on an equal footing with her, with the addition of that deferential respect that every well-bred man owes to a woman, especially an elderly one.

Not expecting to keep Bakunin a long time with her, and wishing in some way or other to attach him to the house (she somehow could not exist without keeping people under her thumb), she even hinted at the possibility of marriage between him and a relative of her own, who was then quite young. Ivan Mikhaylovich consented to this, he was really sincerely in love with the girl and, simply for love of her, he continued to attend to Barbara Petrovna's affairs until 1849. That year, when he had obtained the girl's consent to be his wife at some future time, he left Barbara Petrovna, and went as a special attaché to Count Arsen Alexey Andreyevich Zakrevsky.[1]

Barbara Petrovna's anger was intense, and all intercourse with Bakunin was strictly forbidden.

Esteeming the memory of Ivan Mikhaylovich and his sisters, who were always kind and affectionate towards me, I take this opportunity of clearing up a mistake that has crept into one of the stories about Bakunin, where he, under the imaginary name of Benkendorff, is represented in a very humble position, standing near the lintel of the door, and enduring some impossible treatment from Barbara Petrovna. He was too good, too much of a gentleman to put up with any such insults. It is possible that Barbara Petrovna did box her manager's ears, but even if that were so, the mistake in the name is certain.

In September, 1847, Barbara Petrovna wrote to me about the cholera that was drawing near. The tone of the few lines in which she speaks of it is rather mocking and sarcastic ; further on in her letter she mentions

---

[1] 1783-1865. Governor General of Moscow from 1848-1859.

things that have no connection with cholera, and the whole letter is generally cheerful, showing a very healthy frame of mind, without any fear.

Meanwhile, the epidemic that had threatened in 1847, reached us in 1848, and acted with incredible strength and speed from the beginning. It literally mowed its victims down, one by one ; you might easily see some perfectly healthy man at two o'clock in the afternoon, and at five you might hear that he was dead.

It is extraordinary that this terrible complaint never caused any fear to us young people, that is, to me, to Slavitskaya, mamma's niece, and to my young governess, Vera Nikolayevna Domelunkin.

Not to mention Barbara Petrovna! As a rule she was not afraid of anything or anybody ; it even seemed to me that she, conscious of her importance and her exalted position, was convinced that the cholera would not dare to touch her!

We lived in our usual way ; the same order, and the same drives after dinner, Barbara Petrovna in an open landau, and we, young people, either on horseback or in a cabriolet. As though we wanted to defy the illness, we all three, of course without Barbara Petrovna's knowledge, swallowed dessert consisting of berries and fruit, and an incredible amount of vegetables. What, oh! what did we not eat?

I suppose that such heroism was communicated to us by Barbara Petrovna, who would not allow even a hint as to the possibility of any fear of the cholera. She often talked to us about the epidemic in 1830, and of how bored she was at having to spend several days in quarantine.

All this clearly shows that Barbara Petrovna had a

really strong mind, and that, to her, any kind of cowardice open to ridicule was unthinkable.

At the end of July the epidemic began to die down. The Feast of the Assumption came, and mamma decided to prepare for the Sacrament. The service took place at home, in her oratory. The Spasskoye church was rather cramped, and Barbara Petrovna wanted to receive Holy Communion at home. For this purpose the Holy Elements were brought from the church.

On the 6th of August, after the words "draw near to God in faith and fear," the bells pealed triumphantly, and the priest came out of the church with the Holy Sacrament, and went to the house, where, in her spacious oratory, Barbara Petrovna awaited him.

Behind the priest, by an order given beforehand, followed the people, that is, the aristocracy of the house and office.

They all entered the oratory which was glittering with a great quantity of old, rich family icons.

The priest put the Holy Elements on the table prepared for them, and turned to Barbara Petrovna.

"Do you come to confession, madame?"

"Hear my confession, Father!" and she crossed herself.

"Let everyone go out" . . . the priest turned to the people.

"It isn't necessary," said Barbara Petrovna firmly.

There was confusion, some went to the door, others hesitated.

"Stay! All of you remain!" cried Barbara Petrovna, turning round and confronting them.

"But it is a rule of the church that confession must be made to the father confessor in private," protested the priest gently.

"But I want to make my confession before them all."

"Really, that isn't possible," said the confessor, rather more firmly.

"And I say that it is!" said Barbara Petrovna loudly, and she took the book from the priest's hands.

Father Alexis (I don't know whether he is still alive) was young then—he had only just been appointed; now he lost courage, and was silent. He knew very well that, with her power, her wealth, her connections, and her acquaintance with the bishop, his patroness could do him a great injury, if she presented the facts in quite another light . . . so he gave in.

Then Barbara Petrovna, aloud and clearly, read the prayer "Ruler of Mankind," and having finished she stood facing the people: "I ask for forgiveness," said she, and she bowed in three directions.

"Now, administer the Sacrament, Father!"

When the priest had read the Communion prayer, everyone without exception, bowed to the ground.

The other day I received a letter from Agatha, which reminded me of yet another event in her sorely tried life with Barbara Petrovna. This episode relates to the year 1845, but as it is relevant, but at the same time quite different from the previous story, I have put it in my reminiscences, in that place in my manuscript where I came across the letter from Polyakov's wife:—

After going to see her son in the summer of 1845, Barbara Petrovna, in December of that year, sent Polyakov to Petersburg, to find out whether Nicholas Sergeyevich was really married or not.

Polyakov was sorry for his young master, to whom his mother would not send any money, and who was supporting his family by office work, and by giving lessons : he concealed the real state of affairs from his mistress.

But Barbara Petrovna had relatives and friends in Petersburg. Among them was one family in which one of the daughters was hopelessly in love with Nicholas Sergeyevich. The mother of this girl pursued the son of the rich Madame Turgenev jealously, counting on being able, with her help, to effect a breach between Nicholas and Anna Yakovlevna, whose marriage was not yet officially known. With this aim in view, she wrote to Barbara Petrovna, informing her that her son Nicholas was living as a married man with Anna Yakovlevna, to the great scandal of all their relatives and friends in Petersburg.

This letter arrived soon after Polyakov's return, when he had assured his mistress that Nicholas Sergeyevich was living alone as a bachelor.

Barbara Petrovna flew into an indescribable fury. With the letter in her hand she went out of her room into the adjoining room, called " the mistress's study," and in a voice of thunder shouted: —

" Polyakov ! "

Poor Andrew Ivanovich, white as death, appeared.

" You have deceived me ! You have lied to me ! " said Barbara Petrovna hoarsely, and not giving Polyakov time to utter even a word of excuse, she seized an immense, heavy crutch, that same historic crutch with which her uncle, Ivan Ivanovich Lutovinov, in his warehouse, rapped on his money bags. (See *Three Portraits*.) In her fit of rage, Barbara Petrovna did not even feel its weight, and began to swing it round her steward's head. A moment more and the unfortunate Polyakov would probably have been killed ; but just in time, Nicholas Nikolayevich, her brother-in-law, who was then living at Spasskoye, hurried in.

He rushed hastily up to his sister-in-law, and caught

her hand. Barbara Petrovna fell on the divan. Nicholas Nikolayevich signed to Polyakov to go, and he himself went for some water.

When he returned, Barbara Petrovna took the glass from his hand, looked at him, and in a heavy voice said: —

"Thank you . . . you have saved us both."

The following day an order came from the office, banishing Polyakov to the distant village of Topsky, to be a mere clerk, not a chief steward.

This time it would have been dangerous not to carry out the order.

Polyakov was banished, leaving his wife who was pregnant, very ill, distracted by the separation from her husband, and by her mistress's anger which might yet turn into something worse. So passed the winter. Often and often I saw tears in Agatha's eyes as she fixed them on the icons, whose aid she seemed to be imploring to end her trouble.

God heard her prayer.

But who can explain how it happened ? How can one understand Barbara Petrovna, who, to find out whether her servants drank, pretended to be dying. . . . Barbara Petrovna who in 1849 made her confession aloud, before all the people, and compelled the young confessor to submit to her sovereign will . . . and the Barbara Petrovna who, on this day, gave such proof of kindheartedness and Christian humility!

Easter was drawing near, that same Easter which we were not allowed to celebrate. During Holy Week Barbara Petrovna fasted; on Maundy Thursday I went with her to church for Communion. We had stood through most of the service, the Communion hymn was being sung, when suddenly, Barbara Petrovna went out into the porch, and the astonished footmen both followed her.

"Alexis! Drive away!" she called to her old coachman.

"Home!"

On arriving home, she got out of the carriage, and, still in her fur coat, went with swift steps to her dressing room, where she found Agatha.

Barbara Petrovna stopped straight in front of her, bowed to her, touching the floor with two fingers:—

"Forgive me!"—she said in a loud voice—" at Easter your husband shall be here!"

Agatha Simyonovna threw herself on her knees before her mistress and, with tears of joy, thanked her, and Barbara Petrovna returned to the church and partook of Holy Communion with a clear conscience.

In May, 1848, while in Moscow at school, I received a letter, in which Barbara Petrovna wrote that she was expecting her sons at Spasskoye in the summer. She especially wanted Ivan Sergeyevich, though she was not very well disposed towards him, because he had remained in France at the time of, and after, the February revolution. However, her expectations were not realised, her sons did not come; but the hope alone of once again seeing her favourite had a beneficial effect on Barbara Petrovna. For a little while she was again kinder and more considerate. On Polyakov and his wife, who were favourites of Ivan Sergeyevich, she showered benefits; she joked with them, gave them advice, and chatted cheerfully with them, and once she sent for his wife to inquire about her health.

On Agatha's reply: "Thank God, I am well, madam," Barbara Petrovna continued:—

"I sent for you because I wanted to say that if you

again give birth to a daughter, call her Katherine in honour of my late mother, and in addition, I will allow you to nurse the coming child yourself for a whole year."

Agatha could scarcely believe her ears, and kissed her mistress's hand in gratitude for such unexpected happiness.

Chapter Twelve

BARBARA PETROVNA BUYS A HOUSE FOR HER SON

In January, 1849, her appeal to her sons to return was renewed. I received letters from Barbara Petrovna two or three times a week, and in nearly every one of them, she expressed the hope of having everyone with her in the summer. Bakunin, who had been relieved of his duties, was in disgrace. A faint hope was held out to Nicholas Sergeyevich of consent to his marriage. And six hundred roubles were sent to Ivan Sergeyevich for his journey.

At the beginning of June I was taken to Spasskoye for the holidays. Since May there had been much talk, and preparations for the arrival of the young masters.

The wing was made like new, the flower beds in front of the house gave promise of the most varied shades of verdure and blossom ; the orange trees, already in bud, were arranged round the balcony in immense green tubs; on the other side of the house, the Spanish cherries and reine-claude plum trees had been brought out of the forcing sheds, and covered with a huge net to protect them from the sparrows.

"Set them near the house," said Barbara Petrovna. "Vanya is terribly fond of fruit, and from my window I shall enjoy seeing him eat it."

And in the fruit storing sheds were abundant quantities of seeds for the peach trees, that, at the end of August, would be ready to take the place of the plums and cherries.

On the house waved a flag with the Turgenev coat of arms on one side, and the Lutovinov on the other. It announced that Barbara Petrovna was at home, and would be pleased to receive visitors. When the flag was lowered it meant that she did not want to see anybody.

Once, when out driving, Barbara Petrovna noticed the place where formerly there had been a shallow pond, and remembered that on it her children, when quite small, had been allowed to sail their boat, and had got no little pleasure from it.

In 1849 this place was just a large, dry ditch, overgrown with grass, and bordered by silver poplars.

This ditch was ordered to be cleaned out at once, and on the side near the high road a pillar was to be erected, on one side of which the mistress ordered Nicholas Fedoseyev, a painter brought up in the house (he was also a decorator), to represent a hand stretched out, with one finger pointing, and on the other side an inscription, in French of course :—

"*Ils reviendront.*"

Everything was done punctually, except "they will return." That could not be done. Nicholas Sergeyevich wrote to his mother, in the most affectionate and respectful manner, saying that he was ready to devote his whole life and strength to her service, if only she would agree to his marriage.

Ivan Sergeyevich also wrote a touching letter saying that he was ready to return if only his mother would send him some money for his journey, because the six hundred roubles that he had received had not been enough to pay his debts for the three years during which he had not received anything from her.

Barbara Petrovna answered neither letter.

My reminiscences are nearing the end of 1849, a very memorable year in the Turgenev family.

I was then sixteen years old. My childish carefree day to day existence was then exchanged for many bitter days, and reflections that never left me until mamma's death.

I began to consider more and more deeply and seriously my strange position in Barbara Petrovna's house. I enjoyed every comfort and luxury, and her own children, far away from her, were then in want.

In addition to what had been spent on my education, I was granted for my own expenditure an income from a whole estate, Kholodovo, which was thus described in the office books: "Estate of the young Barbara Niko-layevna Bogdanovich Lutovinov."

This was not a little trouble to me, and afterwards had an influence on my relations with Barbara Petrovna's sons.

Also I had begun to look upon some of mamma's actions with less patience and tolerance, and if I had not yet decided to say anything, she must have read in my eyes that protest which I could with difficulty restrain.

When Barbara Petrovna saw the affection that all her servants felt for me, she constantly tried to pick a quarrel with someone about me, reprimanding them, and probably endeavouring in this way to turn them against me.

All these things made my life almost unbearable. Of course, youth, and the heedlessness peculiar to it, were sometimes responsible for moments of unclouded joy, but some word or other, or a look—and again there returned all the bitterness of a weak, helpless condition, and the impossibility of any kind of aid.

We had an old cook, whom Barbara Petrovna herself valued; no-one else could please her, and no-one could make anything to her taste as well as he. Once, when I had returned from boarding school, I was dining alone with Alexandra Nikolayevna Medvyedeva, the sick nurse and housekeeper; mamma was not well and had ordered her dinner for six o'clock.

When it was taken to her and I went in:—

"Well, and what did you have for dinner to-day?" asked Barbara Petrovna. I told her, but unfortunately I praised the fresh cabbage soup.

"Let me taste it," she demanded.

When the plate containing the unfortunate soup was handed to her, she raised the spoon to her lips, and suddenly threw it on the floor in disgust.

"What sort of rubbish is this! Call Saveliy!"

The cook came in, in his dazzling white cook's uniform.

The usual questions followed: "What is this? What does it mean?" and the poor old man stood there hesitating, not knowing what to answer. Then came rebukes, threats, and a whole stream of condolences about me:—

"My poor girl," began Barbara Petrovna gently "after studying and working, to come home hungry, and to be given such rubbish! It's enough to make her ill!" And again an uproar.

I ran into another room. Such a scene was not the first. My cup of grief and sorrow overflowed, sobs came into my throat.

"Oh, God! Why such torture?" burst from me.

"Barbie!" I heard from the bedroom.

I entered. She fixed a threatening look on me which drew me to the table; but I hadn't got to it when a large crystal jug was thrown full in my face.

I ducked, and, missing me, the jug was smashed to atoms, and only one of the flying pieces of glass hit my plait.

"The carriage!" shouted Barbara Petrovna. "Take her to school!"

While the horses were being harnessed, I stood before her in tears, and listened to the usual reproaches for ingratitude, and for my defence of the serfs, who, accord-ing to her, were dearer to me than she was herself.

When it was announced that the carriage was ready, I made a step as if to go to her and ask her pardon, but she threateningly stopped me with the word: " Away! " and after that I did not come home for a whole week, and was not allowed to see mamma.

The boarding school took the place of my former ban-ishment to the greenhouse or the winter garden.

Because I loved Barbara Petrovna her displeasure was torture to me; however, my lessons and my friends, in fact, freed me from continual fear and oppression.

At the beginning of September Nicholas Sergeyevich arrived, and, at last, his mother allowed him to marry, but on condition that he gave up his work, removed to Moscow, and took upon himself the management of all her estates. In return for this all kinds of benefits were again promised.

Alexandra Mikhaylovna Medvyedeva, Barbara Pet-rovna's nurse and housekeeper, was appointed to look for a house to be sold near Ostozhenka. Barbara Petrovna intended to buy it in her son's name, in order to settle him there with his wife.

Such a house was found at Prechinstenka, adjoining the depot.

Having signed the preliminary agreement, Nicholas Sergeyevich pointed out to Mme. Medvyedeva several repairs and alterations needing to be done in the new house, and, having received his mother's blessing and a small sum of money for the journey, he hurried to Peters-burg to break the good news to his wife.

He resigned the service, and only awaited news from Moscow in order to move into his new dwelling.

But after her son's departure Barbara Petrovna became more and more morose, and never said a word about her

son or the house. Once Mme. Medvyedeva said hesitatingly that the owner wanted to complete the sale of the
house, and asked for payment. To this, Barbara Petrovna,
after remaining silent for a while, answered:—

" In time! "

Meanwhile, letter after letter came from Nicholas
Sergeyevich; he asked what he should do; would everything be ready soon? In order not to distress Nicholas
Sergeyevich, and hoping for a more favourable turn of
the affair, Madame Medvyedeva did not send any word
to Petersburg.

But for me at that time, there were new frocks from
Madame Ladrague, and a still better piano, a Tischner,
was bought for me for eight hundred roubles; for my
drives, a very handsome open carriage with two folding
seats was procured, and so that I should have someone
to accompany me wherever I went, because Barbara Petrovna herself never went out, Sophy Nikolayevna Schröder
was engaged, not as a governess, but as *dame de cam-
pagnie ;* she was a woman of the world and of imposing
appearance, and was paid an excellent salary, in view of
the fact that her dress had to correspond to mine. Again,
for me, every indulgence and luxury, while Nicholas
Sergeyevich in Petersburg waited in vain from day to
day for news of the house that had not yet been bought.

I continued to go to school for a few lessons. One evening at the end of October, on returning home, I was
extremely surprised at the mysterious look of the servant
who helped me out of the carriage.

" Young lady," he whispered, " will you go into the
office for a moment? Leon Ivanovich has a letter there
for you."

What could it be? I had no correspondence secret
from Barbara Petrovna. Curiosity and the fear of something extraordinary were mixed up in my head, but all

the same, I had to go to mamma first, to answer her questions about my lessons, and tell her what had been set for the next day.

Unfortunately a French composition had been set, which I always had to write out in her room, and read the rough draft to her. " For a woman, an elegant style is essential," said she.

But as well as the unlucky composition, I had to play my scales, the Dnieper cataract, and some nocturnes.

But the letter was still lying there, and my guess as to who could have sent it, occupied my thoughts so much that I could not think about anything else.

I set to work on my composition, I can't remember the subject, but at that time young ladies usually cultivated their style on " sunset, the sun and moon, or friendship." But this time I was in such a hurry to finish, that I tore several sheets of paper, and also wrote very badly, for which I got two rebukes, the first from Barbara Petrovna, the other from my teacher who said: " A very careless composition ! "

But every trouble comes to an end. I went into the office and Leon Ivanovich handed me a letter. It was from Nicholas Sergeyevich.

Not suspecting anything unfavourable to himself, he was surprised that he had not received any answer from Madame Medvyedeva, enquired anxiously about his mother's health, asked me to make certain arrangements with regard to the house, and undertake all postal expenses until he arrived.

Generally Nicholas Sergeyevich had treated me rather coldly. He rarely caressed me when I was a child, and then only in his mother's presence. And on his next arrival, that is three weeks after receiving this letter, he treated me rather harshly and scornfully. But afterwards, the former unfriendly relations between us came to an end, and they became most sincere and friendly, and remained so until his death. When I happened to be in Moscow, his house was always my home.

But at that time, we were anything but friends, so that his secret letter, and the trust shown in me, were very pleasant.

What could I answer? What could I do?

Mamma was silent, the house was not bought; that is what I had to tell him, adding for his comfort that perhaps everything would turn out well, that mamma's anger would be changed to kindness; I advised him to have a little patience, and not annoy his mother by any kind of displeasure about her letters.

Nicholas Sergeyevich was very impatient.

But someone else as well as myself had informed him of all that was happening to us; the owner of the house was threatening to sell it to someone else, because Barbara Petrovna had not paid for it, and had not completed the sale. Probably someone had seized the opportunity of telling him about the piano and carriage that had been bought for me. I inferred this, because soon afterwards I received from Nicholas Sergeyevich, in French, a second secret communication, but bitter, despairing, and with his former sarcastic insinuations.

2nd November, 1849.

Mademoiselle:

Thanking you for your kind letters, and the favour you have shown in punctually fulfilling my little commissions, I hasten to tell you that the delay caused by Mme. Sessarewsky in connection with the new purchase (not yet completed) has plunged me in gloomy despair.

Without completely changing my plan of action, I am cruelly forced to modify it, that is to say, I shall come to Moscow alone, and stay in my garret, and as soon as the papers[1] are in my hands, I shall go to the country, not to Spasskoye—that is forbidden, not to Kholodovo— that belongs to you . . . not to any of mamma's estates . . . moreover these would not be a home . . . but I shall pitch my tent at Turgenevo, where, a new Don Quixote, I will build a hovel, and there vegetate where, at least, I shall be in my own home. As I have just told Alexandra Mik-haylovna, I thank God that I have not left Petersburg.

Can you imagine anything more absurd, anything more à la K——sky. My furniture pell-mell on the Moscow pavement, my wife shut out and exiled, alone in Peters-burg in an empty flat, and I everywhere and nowhere, without a sou according to B——sky, lodging at B—— in a hut!

Do not all these things, this throwing my cap over the windmill, this careless what-does-anything-matter, the manners of a comic opera colonel of Hussars, fit me like a glove?[2]

Decidedly I shall become quite mad, having been half mad from my birth. It is with death and shame in my soul that I remain, Mademoiselle (if you still wish it)

Your

Nicholas Turgenev.

Having read this letter I shed tears. Frankly I own that these tears were not caused by sympathy for Nicholas

---

1 Papers: when the Turgenev father died, his estate, the village of Turgenevo, in the province of Tula, Cherny district, was left in charge of Barbara Petrovna as mother and guardian. Her children, always respectful and obedient, and never thinking that she would leave them without money, never claimed their lawful right to their father's estate, and it was only in 1850 when Barbara Petrovna had compelled her son to leave the service, and was also intending to deprive him of everything else, that Nicholas Sergeyevich was forced to procure the papers necessary to provide him with means of support for his family and himself.

2 The last part of the letter and the names inserted, refer to me. And I alone understand all that was sarcastic and insulting, written there between the lines.

Sergeyevich, but by those insults and taunts that I read in, and between the lines.

How was I guilty ? Why did he reproach me for Kholodovo, which I hadn't wanted and hadn't asked for ; it belonged to me by Barbara Petrovna's wish, without my having any legal right to it.

When I became a little calmer and had finished crying about the undeserved insults that I alone understood in the letter, I again began to be sorry for Nicholas Serge-yevich, and also for our dear Ivan Sergeyevich, about whom we were all continually anxious; there he was in a foreign land, and not a *sou* from his mother !

Mme. Medvyedeva and I began to consider what we could do to help, and we thought of the following.

The next day, Mme. Medvyedeva, under the pretext of shopping, got Barbara Petrovna's permission to go out for an hour or two during the morning. I had to go to school, but in addition to the school and the shopping, we set out, armed with Nicholas Sergeyevich's letters to Barbara Petrovna's relative and friend, Anna Ivanovna Kireyevsky.

Of all Barbara Petrovna's relations and friends, I think that Mme. Kireyevsky was the only one whom she at all liked and respected; she evidently looked upon her as almost her equal !

Much of her agreeable relations with Barbara Petrovna depended on Anna Ivanovna's unusual cleverness, and her ease of manner, not often met with in those of her acquaintances not subject to her authority.

Anna Ivanovna Kireyevsky, although she was well disposed towards Barbara Petrovna, yet fully maintained her own dignity ; she cleverly and skilfully knew how to avoid a collision, and now and then, if she could not subdue her proud and intractable cousin, she did, in some things, make her agree with her, and that was something.

It was to her that Mme. Medvyedeva and I went for advice. We drew up an elaborate scheme by which Barbara Petrovna might be persuaded in some way or other to complete the purchase of the house.

Two days after our secret visit to her, Mme. Kireyevsky came to see us in the evening.

For a long time she and Barbara Petrovna talked about various things, exchanging news; suddenly in the very midst of the conversation, Anna Ivanovna burst into a fit of laughter.

Astonished, Barbara Petrovna looked at her inquiringly.

"*Pensez donc, cousine,*" began Mme. Kireyevsky, still laughing (the whole conversation was in French), "Just imagine, cousin, what absurd gossip is being circulated all over Moscow! Suddenly I am informed in the house of one of my acquaintances, that Mme. Sessarevsky is going to sell her house to someone" (here Anna made a sign as if trying to recollect), "I've forgotten to whom ... in a word, to someone, but not to you, and just think of it, for a perfectly ridiculous reason; I am told that you refuse to complete the purchase!

"When I was told that you had refused to pay money, I, of course, contradicted it. I was even grieved for you when I heard such nonsense! Such folly! I defended you warmly! Was it likely that you would do such a thing? To promise to give your son a house because you wanted him to be nearer to you, and then to cry off! To break your promise, your given word! Was it likely that you would do such a thing?"

Barbara Petrovna listened to all this, and was indignant herself at such gossip.

Anna Ivanovna's lesson bore fruit. Mme. Medvyedeva was soon sent for.

"Tell me please, Sasha," Barbara Petrovna questioned, as if she felt surprised and insulted ... "when did I say that I refused to pay for Nicholas's house? Did I say anything like that? Certainly I delayed a little, but I was really very much worried and distressed," and at this she raised her handkerchief to her eyes. " To-morrow morning," she continued, " go to Mme. Sessarevsky and tell her that this very week I will complete everything. My agent shall go to her with the money."

Then, everyone tried to strike while the iron was hot; within two days all the formalities were completed, the house was acquired, and by deed of gift handed over to Nicholas Sergeyevich.

I hastened to inform him of this, in very dry and ceremonious letters.

But after all, Barbara Petrovna's inner struggle with regard to all this was not without cost. She really was not at all well, and was not able to write herself. At her dictation, and with her signature alone, I sent to Nicholas Sergeyevich in her name a most affectionate letter, in which she invited him: "Come and live in your new house, in the nest which your loving mother has built for you." But in the middle of the letter was the command " if necessary, find a Frenchwoman, the wife of a Turgenev ought to speak French well."

At the end of November, Nicholas Sergeyevich with his wife, his sister-in-law Katerina Yakovlevna, still a young girl, and a Frenchwoman, Mme. Chevalier, removed to Moscow.

The morning after his arrival he came to see us. He met me in a kind and friendly manner, and from that moment until the end of his life, he was always kind and considerate to me.

His mother received him rather dryly. She did not ask about his wife, and did not mention her. At first she was not in any hurry to establish her son and daughter-in-law on a proper footing. But later, she sent him male and female servants, horses, carriages and a coachman, and this led to a new expression with us: "that house, in that house, from that house."

Once, someone was imprudent enough to call Nicholas and his wife "the young masters."

"Who are these young masters?" asked Barbara Petrovna sternly. . . . "Has my second son Ivan arrived? You have only one young master here, my son Nicholas."

Barbara Petrovna did not like her daughter-in-law, and did not receive her, but she never spoke slightingly about her to anyone. She was too proud to admit strangers to her family affairs.

Her intimate side was scarcely known to anyone except me, Agatha, and Mme. Medvyedeva.

The fourth of December drew near, Barbara Petrovna's name day, and mine. On the occasion of my sixteenth birthday, I had been promised a dance in the evening. Barbara Petrovna specially emphasised to her son that she would invite "everybody."

As a rule she liked to nourish him on false hopes. Everybody was invited but not "all."

Nicholas Sergeyevich was ordered to come early, because he was, after his mother, the principal host.

It was painful for Nicholas Sergeyevich to be at his mother's, among such a crowd of people, alone, without his wife. But he had to stay. Of course he did not consider himself the host. He was generally a great misanthropist in society, but now, in the somewhat false position of a married man without his wife, he was still more out of his element.

And we young people who were dancing and whirling about never even thought that among us, and in the midst of our general merriment, was a profoundly miserable man, and that that man was none other than our host.

At the climax of the evening, Nicholas Sergeyevich abruptly left the drawing room, where his mother's dumb command, which he had read in her sharp, expressive eyes had forced him to remain.

He went out into the hall, and stood between two pillars, with his arms crossed on his chest. Even now I can see his fine figure. He was in evening dress, dressed with great care, and was very handsome, that is, remarkably well turned out, "gentleman like." There was a rather sardonic, sarcastic smile on his face as he looked at the couples dancing near him.

Many young ladies turned their attention to him, some were even fascinated by him, and called him by the nickname " Rochester," at that time a great hero and ideal.

Time went by until Twelfth Night, and neither Christmas nor New Year's Day, those festive days on which families and friends are united, brought any change in the unfriendly relations between Barbara Petrovna and her daughter-in-law.

Anna Yakovlevna, having formed a circle of relatives and friends, went out often, and Barbara Petrovna was pleased to hear that she was well dressed, and well spoken of.

But she continued to torment and embarrass her son.

She demanded that he should come to see her every day at eleven o'clock in the morning, and she kept him until three or four o'clock, either for business or conversation.

She also demanded that he should come in the evening. At the same time she would often say to him:—

" Have a little patience, the time will come when I will do everything for you that you want." She gave him hope which she immediately afterwards pitilessly destroyed.

By chance I have kept one of my notes to Nicholas

Sergeyevich with his answer on the back of it, reminding me of one of Barbara Petrovna's.

It was probably during the Christmas festival; I wrote to him by his mother's order, that she expected him at two o'clock, not eleven. He answered in English, " Very well ! " I told mamma that I had received an answer.

" Where is the note? " she asked.

I gave it to her. " Write this," and she dictated the following:—

" *We shall have friends here this evening between six and eleven. Mamma expects you* all."

The last word was underlined by Barbara Petrovna herself.

I got a secret answer to this note from Nicholas Sergeyevich. He wrote to me in English: *" I don't understand this, and beg you to explain."*

How could I explain? It was a complete puzzle. As I knew Barbara Petrovna better, I advised him in a secret letter not to draw any favourable conclusion from this, but to wait until evening, when there might be some fresh arrangement.

I was not mistaken: this arrangement followed. At five o'clock Barbara Petrovna called one of the boys standing near her door, and ordered:—

" Go to ' that house ' and ask Nicholas Sergeyevich to come here at once."

The boy was rushing away, but I managed to slip a note into his hand, on which was written " come alone." And a good thing I did!

Because Barbara Petrovna's conversation that evening with Mme. Medvyedeva showed very clearly that had Nicholas Sergeyevich done otherwise, he would have done quite the wrong thing.

But his position in Moscow began to be rather critical. His mother had given him a house, and servants to look after his family, also horses, but she had not given him any money.

At first Nicholas Sergeyevich lived on what he had received from the sale of some of his Petersburg property; but the upkeep of the carriages and horses cost a good deal, and his modest funds could not last long. Once he told his mother that he hadn't any money, and she replied : —

"Wait! Your brother Ivan will soon be here. I will settle an estate on you, and all shall be yours."

Nicholas Sergeyevich dared not insist, and he was obliged to borrow.

But she dressed me more and more richly, and even gave me diamond crosses and necklaces and solitaires, estimated at twenty-eight thousand roubles.

One fine day Barbara Petrovna wanted me to try on all these riches, and she dressed me up herself.

"You shall be married in this, and now, lock it up in your jewel case, and carry the key round your neck," said she.

But when Nicholas Sergeyevich asked for anything, she replied that she had no money. All in good time!

What Barbara Petrovna's object could have been in behaving in such a manner, is a mystery to us all to this day. She loved me—of that I am fully convinced—although in her own way; every letter to me is alone sufficient proof; but she loved her children much more, especially Ivan.

Nearly every day from the beginning of February she said : —

"I must send Vanya some money," and day by day she put off, for any sort of trivial reason; and so it was that for several days Barbara Petrovna would be pleased to forget all about it, and then say : —

" Ah! I've forgotten again! I must send some money abroad to-morrow."

Just at the beginning of spring Barbara Petrovna fell rather seriously ill. Inozemtsev visited her every day. Alexandra Mikhaylovna scarcely ever left her bedroom.

One morning mamma called me before I went to school.

"Don't go to school to-day," she said. "I can't spare Sasha. You alone must go to the office at Zänker, and take the money to be sent to Ivan. Remember that you go alone. Don't be thoughtless, don't lose it, be careful to get a receipt, and bring it to show me."

At the beginning of this lecture my heart beat with joy.

At last! I thought.

Until the carriage was ready, I was terrified lest Barbara Petrovna should again change her mind.

The carriage came, I went into the bedroom and was entrusted with a package. I do not know how I refrained from running downstairs with it. Fortunately I remembered that, in mamma's eyes, I was now a responsible being, entrusted with a large sum of money, and not a seventeen year old girl, nearly off her head with joy.

It was quite a long way from Ostozhenka to the Zänker banking office. All the way I was looking out of the carriage window, afraid of being pursued, because Barbara Petrovna had again changed her mind.

The coachman to whom I continually shouted: " Quicker, please, quicker! " was rather offended.

" What's the matter with you, young lady? Don't I know how to drive? Surely there isn't a fire! "

But my imagination was so active that I could not get rid of my feeling of fear, and when I went into the office, my hands were trembling as I handed over the packet to one of the clerks.

" For M. Turgenev, in Paris. Quickly, please, quickly! "

The clerk looked at me in surprise, and offered me a chair.

At last I thankfully took the receipt home, and even received undeserved encouragement.

"You must accustom yourself to this, get into the habit," said Barbara Petrovna, "I am getting weaker and weaker every day, soon you will have to be my secretary, take on all my correspondence, and do my errands."

In the interval between sending the money and Ivan Sergeyevich's arrival, a dreadful accident happened to Nicholas and his wife.

They were driving in the Petrovsky park, the horses bolted, and the carriage was smashed to pieces on a road covered with a layer of broken stones. Nicholas Sergeyevich was considerably bruised about the shoulders and legs. Anna Yakovlevna fell on her head and face on the stones, and received a very bad wound in the head. They were carried, apparently dead, into someone's summer house.

Later in the evening, when they had been taken home, news of this accident was quickly brought to Barbara Petrovna.

Porphyry Timofeyevich was sent as quickly as possible to "that house." We did not sleep at all that night, and messengers were continually sent to inquire what Theodore Ivanovich Inozemstev said. Were his patients in danger? Had they fallen asleep? Barbara Petrovna was terribly upset, all the more because she herself was not well enough to go to them.

When she was a little better she sent word to her son that she was going to call and see him, but she made him understand that she wanted to see him alone.

She sat for quite a long time with her son, and on leaving she went to the closed door of the adjoining

room, where Anna Yakovlevna lay, and said in a loud
voice : —

" I hope that you will soon be quite well."

Meanwhile, from day to day, we were expecting Ivan
Sergeyevich, hoping that his kindliness and affection
would have a beneficial effect on his mother.

In one of his letters he told her how pleased he would
be to see her again, also his brother, now married, and
the others connected with her, but he regretted that he
would not have the pleasure of seeing his uncle, Nicholas
Nikolayevich, and that his absence from his mother's
house would be perceptibly painful. When Ivan Sergeyevich went abroad in 1846 Nicholas Nikolayevich had
not yet finally broken with his sister-in-law.

Barbara Petrovna herself did not write to her brother-
in-law, but she left it to me to inform him of his favourite
nephew's arrival. As she did not give me any instructions
as to the tone of my letter, I took it as permission to write
to Nicholas Nikolayevich, expressing those same feelings
of love, esteem and gratitude with which my letters to
him were always filled.

I soon received an answer. His letter gives the best
proof of the unusual goodness of this man, of his love for
Ivan Sergeyevich, and his unbounded attachment and
devotion to Barbara Petrovna, who so cruelly threw him
over because of his new family life.

" Christ is risen.

I congratulate you, my dear little friend Barbara. From
my soul I wish you all God's blessings.   I thank you,
my angel, for your welcome news of Ivan Sergeyevich's
arrival. I felt as if I had received new life the moment
I got your letter. I cannot explain to you my joy. I
never expected to receive a present so dear to my heart.
I am very glad about Ivan Sergeyevich's return, and

doubly glad for your letter, written doubtless with mamma's consent, and therefore I think that I am not quite cast out of her memory. I dare not bother her with a letter. I beg you, my dear friend, to express my feelings of sincere friendship. I find that I was guilty in much.

Perhaps by my fault, I was the cause of displeasure and even sorrow; that grieves my mind. Not having any other means of relieving my heart of its wounds, I take refuge in the solemn resurrection of our Lord Jesus Christ. On that holy day, reconciliation should take the place of enmity, and in the name of our Saviour we should embrace each other.

Soothe the grief of my mind, and take upon yourself the trouble of giving mamma my good wishes. Kiss her hand, and beg her to pardon me. Your last letter gave me life again; do not deprive me of it; let my peace of mind return. Our life is so brief that we have no time to efface the traces of our guilt. The circumstances of my life are especially difficult and onerous, so that I am deprived of all means of meeting you personally, now or later. I await your answer impatiently.

I remain sincerely,

Your loving Nicholas Turgenev.

1850. April 17th. Village of Yushky."

But this letter, with all its expressions of love and hope for a reconciliation, did not move Barbara Petrovna. I again replied. I wrote that mamma, and all of us, would probably be at Spasskoye, and there, *perhaps*, we should see each other. But there was no invitation from Barbara Petrovna, and not a word from her personally in my letter to Nicholas Nikolayevich.

But this general meeting of us all at Spasskoye was

not destined to take place. The summer was most distressing and bitter for us all. No joyous meetings, no family reunion.

In the Turgenev house a family drama was being played, that still remains in the memory of those who are living, and was a heavy burden on the hearts of those who are dead, to their last moment.

Chapter Thirteen

TROUBLE FOLLOWS A PLEASANT INTERLUDE

In the spring Ivan Sergeyevich was in Petersburg. Circumstances kept him there rather a long time, and that made his mother seriously uneasy.

But at last her Benjamin arrived!

There was no end to her tears and exclamations of joy! Now I met Ivan Sergeyevich not as a child, but as a seventeen year old girl. At our first meeting we embraced each other as of old, but those childish, friendly relations, of course, could not be renewed . . . we had grown apart, and moreover, our years would not permit the former intimacy.

During the first days of the meeting there were continual questions on the mother's side. and continual stories on the son's side. Ivan Sergeyevich was jolly and talkative. He spoke with special pleasure of Count V——ko, and of those people who particularly sympathised with him because of his long absence from Russia.

At first everything went well. Barbara Petrovna was in ecstasy, and the whole house wore a festive appearance. There was talk of a general move to Spasskoye. Ivan Sergeyevich wanted to go there at the beginning of June for the shooting. His mother agreed, and decided to remain in Moscow until that time.

This year Ivan Sergeyevich's circle of acquaintances was considerably enlarged. He was already "known." (I must say, however, that though he was known in Moscow as an author, he was not "known" in our house; there, he was not read.) Invitations were showered on him from all sides, he hardly ever dined at home, but he spent all his mornings until nearly two o'clock with his mother.

It was impossible to ask more; Barbara Petrovna herself did not try to keep him with her any longer; she was satisfied with his mornings. They belonged entirely to her, because her health did not allow her to hold any receptions, and to tell the truth, things were rather dull.

But Ivan Sergeyevich's continual absence from the house was particularly disagreeable to one very charming lady, who formerly, when she was still almost a girl, was the object of Ivan Sergeyevich's youthful, passionate, but hopeless love.

This was a long time ago when he was a boy ; his love did not even flatter the beauty's vanity; she paid no attention to the youth who sighed for her. When, after all these years, Ivan Sergeyevich returned from abroad, he was in all the splendour of his mature good looks, and at the beginning of his fame. A few grey hairs, sprinkled in his head and beard, made his handsome face still more interesting. He was now considered to be important and his attentions and courtly manners were flattering to any woman. The beauty, who had spurned the boy, remembered that this present Turgenev was the man who, as a youth, had sighed for her.

And what woman is not pleased to believe in the charm exercised by her beauty. However, perhaps with the intention of arousing his former love, perhaps from curiosity alone, or even simply with the desire to see Ivan Sergeyevich, and invite him to go and see her, in order to be able to say "Turgenev came to see me"—I cannot exactly determine—but it was evident that this lady's acquaintance with Barbara Petrovna, which had latterly been confined to two or three visits a year, suddenly became of the most friendly kind, her carriage stood oftener and oftener at our door, and her visits were more and more prolonged. Alas! They did not give her what she wanted.

When she arrived in the morning, Ivan Sergeyevich who in a wide frock coat or overcoat was sitting with his mother, rushed hurriedly upstairs to his own room, and did not show himself.

If she arrived at eight o'clock in the evening he was not at home.

After a few failures, the lady decided, under some plausible pretext, to come at a time unknown to the code of society—between six and seven in the evening, considering probably that if Ivan Sergeyevich had dined at home, he would not have had time to go out.

In spite of her being nearly forty, this lady preserved traces of remarkable beauty. Her toilet, not quite in accordance with her years, white muslin dress, pink sash, an expensive black lace cloak on her shoulders, and a three-cornered handkerchief arranged Spanish fashion on her head, so suited her that she could certainly be considered attractive. In the smooth pallor of her face, which had now lost the rosiness of youth, her charming black eyes were made all the more attractive by eyelashes that Barbara Petrovna said were not eyelashes but sun-blinds!

"I have called to see how you are, Barbara Petrovna," said she on entering. . . . "Pardon this country attire. I am going to spend the evening in the park with my sister. And it is so hot that I couldn't put on anything else."

Barbara Petrovna made a sign that she believed her, although it did not escape her penetration that this "country attire" was intentional, and she replied very slyly:—

"You are only all the more beautiful. You remind me of what you were like at seventeen."

But unfortunately she met with a bitter disappointment.

That evening, Ivan Sergeyevich and I had made arrangements to go to the Races, and afterwards to ride in the Park. The horses were already saddled, and my Sophy Nikolayevna Schröder, in hat and gloves, was ready to take her seat in the carriage to accompany us.

Ivan Sergeyevich came down dressed for riding, and with his hat in his hand. He sat down for a quarter of an hour, said a few words of welcome to his mother's guest, and then turned to me: —

"Well now, Barbie, shall we go? It will soon be seven o'clock."

And we got up.

The next morning, mamma began to joke about Ivan Sergeyevich, and laughing, she reproached him for his indifference to his guest's beauty: —

"For a woman bordering on forty, she is still very beautiful. She went to a lot of trouble for you, and you were not very agreeable."

Ivan Sergeyevich sat at his mother's writing table, and sketched something in pencil.

"Yes ! " said he . . . "then I was a boy, and I really suffered. I remember that if she happened to go past me, my heart was ready to burst. That golden time has gone! One does not love in that way now. There is not that youthful ardour . . . not that love which is content with a look . . . with a flower that has fallen from her hair. You pick up that flower, and how happy you are! . . . you want nothing more."

I went up to the table at which he was sitting. In front of him lay a sheet of paper with letters and marks on it. I bent down in order to read it, but I could not make anything out. He himself, seeing my perplexity, read it to me, but only the last four lines:

> Tell me: could I foresee
> That we were fated to be parted,
> And to hate the love
> Long since destroyed.

Like all young girls at that time, I was a lover of verses ; I was very sure that I wanted to keep these ; but Ivan Sergeyevich's handwriting, never distinguished for its legibility, and now in pencil, and on a sheet of paper dotted all over with all kinds of fantastic figures, etc., pleased me less than ever, and I preferred to have these verses copied out ; with this intention, I went into the office and asked the clerk, Leon Ivanovich, to write them for me, which he did, in the clearest and most beautiful handwriting. I have these verses now.

Those verses did not refer to that lady. They probably just came into Ivan Sergeyevich's mind that morning. They were already in print in 1846 and signed T. L.

With this episode ended all that was pleasant during the last months of my life with Barbara Petrovna.

It is painful and distressing to remember and relate all that took place in the days that followed ; the only consolation in this drama was the rare consideration shown by Nicholas and Ivan to their mother. In spite of her cruel mockery, they remained always obedient sons, ready even to be affectionate, if she herself had not repulsed them.

In the month of June Nicholas Sergeyevich's circumstances became more and more straitened.

His and his wife's illnesses, following their accident in the Park, had cost him a good deal of money.

Ivan Sergeyevich also, after visiting his friends and

acquaintances, was not even able to repay their hospitality with a bottle of wine. More than once he got thirty to fifty kopecks from Leon Ivanovich or Porphyry Timofeyevich to pay the cabman who had driven him home.

Ivan Sergeyevich's lack of money, and Nicholas Sergeyevich's desperate need of it, compelled them to speak to their mother.

In the most respectful and affectionate manner they asked her to allow them at least a small income, so that they might know how much they could spend, and not have to bother her about every little thing.

Barbara Petrovna listened to her sons without anger, and quite agreed that it was necessary to allow them a definite income.

Meanwhile, day after day went by, and no arrangement was made—the most complete silence reigned.

Ivan Sergeyevich renewed the conversation:—

"I am not asking for myself so much as for my brother," he said to his mother. "I can manage with my books and translations, but he has nothing! Soon he won't have anything to eat!"

"I will do everything, everything," replied Barbara Petrovna. "You shall both be satisfied."

Actually, that morning an order was sent to Leon Ivanovich, her chief clerk, to write on plain paper two "deeds of gift," by which Barbara Petrovna arranged to give the estate of Sychevo[1] to her son Nicholas, and Kadnoye to her son Ivan.

These deeds of gift were made out at home, without observing any legal formalities.

Her sons came during the morning by her orders; she read the rough draft to them and asked:—

[1] Sychevo belongs now to Madame Malyarevsky, niece of Nicholas Sergeyevich's wife.

" Are you satisfied with me now ? "

Nicholas Sergeyevich was silent, and Ivan answered:—

" Of course, mamma, we shall be satisfied, and we shall be grateful to you, if you will do everything legally."

"What does that mean, legally? " inquired Barbara Petrovna.

"Why should I explain, mamma, you know yourself what it means ; and if you really want to do something for us, you know how to do it."

"I really don't understand you, Jean. What do you want me to do? I am giving each of you an estate.... I do not understand. . . ."

Barbara Petrovna often liked to make use of this expression: I do not understand, especially when she knew very well what was wanted of her.

Nicholas Sergeyevich's silence continued.

Ivan Sergeyevich walked once or twice round the room, and, without saying a word, went out.

"Nicholas, what does all this mean?" Barbara Petrovna, who was already annoyed, turned to her elder son.

Nicholas Sergeyevich got up, tried to say something, and rushed out of the room.

Her sons had occasion to be not only dissatisfied, but hurt by their mother's treatment.

Leon Ivanovich informed them, of course unknown to his mistress, that, that very morning, the bailiffs of both estates had received an order from her by post, to sell quickly, and without waiting for any bargaining, all the corn stored in the barns of the estates which she had given. Another order was sent to the Spasskoye chief manager, to examine for as quick a sale as possible, the corn in the aforementioned estates, and to send the money received from the sale immediately to Moscow, in Barbara Petrovna's own name.

What then remained of the work of the peasants on those " deed of gift " estates?

Not even one grain of corn for future sowing.

Both brothers, their heads down, went out of the house. Ivan Sergeyevich did not return to dinner.

Thirty-three years have elapsed since all this happened. My memory might have been at fault if all that I had seen and heard had not been discussed a hundred times with my friends and my family, and if still earlier, the details of the scenes that follow had not been described in my correspondence with Barbara Petrovna's niece, Madame Slivitskaya. Therefore, every word, even every gesture, has all been vividly preserved in my memory.

Moreover, such scenes can never be forgotten. Those who have had the misfortune to live through any kind of family drama know from experience how the least detail leaves ineffaceable marks on any life, even the idlest, and especially on the mind of one who has herself experienced all the sorrow of a family quarrel.

In this drama, I was an actor and a witness, at an age when every sensation is unusually vivid ; all this had such a great effect on me that it even made me ill.

When her sons had gone, Barbara Petrovna shut herself up in her study with her clerk ; they made a fair copy of the deeds of gift.   That day at five o'clock, mamma ordered me to go to " that house " and tell her sons that she expected them at eight o'clock in the evening.

I found the whole family at dinner ; but by the distressed faces of the brothers, and the red eyes of Nicholas's wife and sister-in-law, it was evident that dinner was nothing but a formality. The dishes were removed almost untouched.

Ivan Sergeyevich was sad, but calm. Nicholas Sergeyevich, always very excitable, was almost tearing his hair as he spoke of his misfortunes.

When I explained the object of my visit, Ivan Sergeyevich asked me if there had been any change in the form of the deeds of gift, and if a lawyer had been sent for.

I told the truth: a fair copy had been made of the deeds of gift, signed by Barbara Petrovna, but there was no lawyer, and when her family adviser, entrusted with her affairs, remarked that such a paper had no legal value, Barbara Petrovna answered: " Rubbish! "

" Then everything is as it was," said Ivan Sergeyevich, as if to himself, and he was anxious to know if mamma guessed that they knew about her order regarding the sale of corn. He, of course, was afraid for Leon Ivanovich, whose life would be a burden to him if his mistress knew that he had told her sons about the orders she had sent by post.

Her sons understood from what I said, that no change for the better could be expected. It was clear that their mother had no intention of giving anything in a legal manner.

At this, Nicholas Sergeyevich's face became even more distressed.

Wringing his hands, and with tears in his eyes, he maintained that at last he would be obliged to remove to Turgenovo,[1] his father's estate. He did not look upon the Prechistenka house as his ; but he considered that he had a legal and moral right to the inheritance from his father. He offered to halve the income with his brother.

" I don't need anything," interrupted Ivan Sergeyevich. " There will scarcely be enough for you, and I can do without it."

Then Nicholas Sergeyevich began to sob. . . .

[1] The estate of the Turgenev father, in the province of Tula, district of Cherny, now belongs to Mme. Malyarevsy, Nicholas's wife's niece.

" Isn't it terrible," said he, " that I gave up the service, and am now without a crust ; terrible that if I assert my right to my inheritance, I must go against mamma! This will be a grievance with mamma, who, until now, has ruled without us over this estate. Who can understand such a thing? And I wanted to be with my brother! To go back to Petersburg," he continued still more despairingly. " To enter the service again! Shame! Shame! What shall I say? What will people say? Mamma is dishonest...."

He did not finish speaking, but threw himself on a chair and covered his face with his hands.

A heavy silence followed, broken by the sobs of Anna Yakovlevna, who was on the point of having a nervous attack.

" Well then, brother, shall we go there? " Ivan Sergeyevich's gentle voice was heard.

" I do not know," said Nicholas Sergeyevich, almost hopelessly.

I timidly advised them to go without fail to mamma at eight o'clock, and even expressed the hope that perhaps there would be a change for the better, although in my own mind I could not imagine it, but I was afraid of a terrible quarrel between mother and sons if they did not carry out her order.

Both promised to come at the appointed time.

" Well then? " Barbara Petrovna met me when I went back to her.

" They will come," I replied.

" Well, how was it there? "

" They were dining when I arrived."

" Did they say anything? " and Barbara Petrovna looked at me with such a threatening, searching look, that I could not endure it. I dropped my eyes.

" Why are you silent? What is it ? " She noticed

my look of confusion. " What's the matter with you? "

This last question was too much. The terrible scene with her sons, during which I had kept back my tears so that I should not arrive home with red eyes, and mamma's present painful questioning, were too much for my nerves.... I felt a thickening in my throat, as if something hot was in it . . . my breath came with such an awful noise that Barbara Petrovna ran to me in alarm. I seized her hand, tried to say something . . . and blood poured out of my mouth.

" Porphyry! Who is there? What is the matter with her ? " shouted Barbara Petrovna.

Mme. Schröder and Mme. Medvyedeva rushed in, and they laid me on a couch.

Then I had to sip the well-known laurel drops ; but this nervous attack spared me any further questioning. Either Barbara Petrovna was sorry for me, or she saw that in my present condition she could hardly get anything out of me . . . so she vented her anxiety on poor Mme. Schröder.

" What is the matter with Barbie now ? " she turned to her. . . . " Surely such a thing hasn't happened for a long time. You ought to know! Has anything of this kind happened in your presence ? "

On receiving a negative answer she continued, still with that same displeasure in her voice:—

" It can't be.... What is the cause today? She was quite well! It must be riding too fast! You don't stop her! You don't look after her! It is your duty...."

And cutting rebukes rained on Mme. Schröder.

Meanwhile, we were all quite convinced that Barbara Petrovna guessed that my attack had been caused by something that had happened in " that house "; she remembered very well that it occurred just at the moment when I was going to tell her something.

Probably, by pouring unjust rebukes on Mme. Schröder, she wanted to force me to tell her the whole truth, and I do not know what would have been the end of it if Porphyry Timofeyevich had not come in and advised fresh air.

"Go out on the balcony!" commanded mamma. I went out and Mme. Schröder followed.

At eight o'clock her sons arrived, but I was on my guard.

It would have been exceedingly unpleasant for me if her sons should suspect that I had repeated their conversation before me to Barbara Petrovna. I was convinced that Barbara Petrovna would try to find out the cause of my sudden illness. And events proved that I was not mistaken.

"What happened at your house?" Barbara Petrovna asked them. "Barbie was not herself at all when she left you . . . she had some sort of fit . . . she was spitting blood. . . . What was it? I do not understand."

"Nothing, mamma, there was nothing, everything was very cheerful there!" I got my word in before either of them had time to answer his mother's question. I stood at the door of the balcony leading into the drawing room where Barbara Petrovna was sitting.

"Be quiet!" she cried out. "I was not asking you! Go away!"

I went out into the hall, considerably calmer. Now both brothers understood that their mother did not know of their conversation and decision.

Ivan Sergeyevich soon followed me. What an expression of kindness and sympathy was on his face! He took me by the hand, and looked inquiringly at me.

I whispered, scarcely audibly: "Afterwards, afterwards!" and pointed to the door of the drawing room, and he returned there.

The table was laid for tea in the hall.

Mme. Medvyedeva carried a cup to Barbara Petrovna ; the servants handed glasses to her sons. From the drawing room could be heard the stirring of spoons and the sound of the packs of cards that Barbara Petrovna was shuffling for Patience. For a little while there was silence.

All that I saw and suffered that day is so vividly imprinted on my memory, and had so great an effect on my whole life, that it is impossible to forget any of it.

Barbara Petrovna spoke first, expatiating on different kinds of tea, some of which she liked, and others that were not to her taste, then she went off into some kind of quite unimportant talk ; her sons answered her briefly. I felt that all three were not thinking about what they were saying ; there was a kind of false note in each speaker's voice.

Mme. Schröder, Mme. Medvyedeva and I sat in the hall. We scarcely moved, we were listening to what was being said in the drawing room, a part of which was reflected in an immense mirror ; this allowed us to see only Barbara Petrovna's white, elegant hands, moving over the table arranging the cards, but Nicholas Sergeyevich, who was sitting on her right, and Ivan, who was sitting at the table opposite his mother, were wholly visible. "There, now, something is going to happen," thought each one of us. But if we had been asked what was going to happen, we would not have known how to answer, but we should have said that it was something dreadful! If at that moment a perfect stranger had come into the hall and looked at us he would, by the expression of our faces alone, by our eyes turned with intensity on the picture reflected in the mirror, have understood that something extraordinary was about to happen, of which we were all terrified.

At last Barbara Petrovna rang.

"Call Leon Ivanovich," she ordered when the servant entered.

"Bring it!" she said shortly to the clerk, when he showed himself at the door.

In a few moments Leon Ivanovich brought two packets, and handed them on a tray to his mistress.

Barbara Petrovna looked at the inscriptions, and she gave one of them to Nicholas Sergeyevich, and the other to Ivan.

A few seconds elapsed ; both held the packets in their hands. Ivan Sergeyevich moved a little further from the table.

"Read them through!" said Barbara Petrovna impatiently.

Her sons obeyed. A rustling of paper was heard in the dead silence reigning in the house.

"Well then, thank me!" and their mother stretched out her right hand to Nicholas and her left to Ivan. Nicholas, as if mechanically, kissed his mother's hand in silence.

Whether Ivan Sergeyevich saw the hand stretched out to him, I do not know ; he sat with his head bent low.

In a few seconds he got up, walked to the open door of the balcony, took a few steps back into the room, again went out on the balcony, and having decided what to do, went quickly to his mother.

"Good night, mamma," said he, quietly as he always spoke, as he spoke when a child, and when a youth, never by a word or a look expressing the bitterness his mother's mockery of them caused him, and he stooped and kissed her hand.

His mother blessed him, as she did all of us every

night, and he went out, quickly went along the hall, not looking at any of us, and soon we heard his step on the stairs . . . he had gone upstairs to the room he occupied there.

Nicholas Sergeyevich had still not recovered. When I went in to say goodnight to mamma, he sat with a kind of dull look on his face. Barbara Petrovna continued to lay out her cards for Patience, but her hands trembled perceptibly, and her frown, and her eyes fixed obstinately on the arrangement of the heaps of cards, witnessed to her anger, until then controlled.

Usually she was anxious about my health; this time she did not even look at me, and during all my life with her, this was the first time such a thing had happened.

Nicholas Sergeyevich got up after me, said the usual "good night, mamma," received her blessing, and went out, but not home—upstairs to his brother.

In the house the lights were put out. Barbara Petrovna retired to her bedroom, and when Mme. Medvyedeva went in as usual to rub her legs, Barbara Petrovna said: "Not necessary!" and waved her away.

Her sons, in Ivan Sergeyevich's room, and in Porphyry Timofeyevich's presence, from whom I heard this, decided to assert their right to inherit their father's estate, not to have any quarrel with their mother, or enter into any explanation, and not to try persuasion or entreaty. But it was understood that they would not go to those estates which had been given to them "on paper," they risked either not being received there as masters, or exposed themselves to a cruel responsibility for those who so received them.

Thus the whole transaction came to an end; her sons, not blaming their mother, would have remained the same towards her, if Barbara Petrovna herself had not forced the gentle Ivan Sergeyevich to tell her all that for long years had been stored in his mind.

Chapter Fourteen

GROWING TENSION

THE following morning Ivan Sergeyevich came to his mother just as usual, inquired about her health, and explained that he was going into the country, that the date for hunting had arrived, and that it was time for her to leave sultry Moscow.

The conversation took place in the drawing room, and I, sitting in the hall, was already rejoicing that all was going happily, without any stormy scenes. Barbara Petrovna's triumph was complete. Her power over her sons was not shaken. She had promised much and done nothing, and neither of her sons had shown any displeasure; they bore her spiteful mockery submissively, and her favourite even came to persuade her, for the sake of her health, to leave Moscow. With all her passion for testing the limits of his patience, she ought to have been satisfied, but she wanted more. In fact she was subdued, not by her son's indignation against her on his own account, but by her kindly, truth loving Benjamin, who could be mildly and patiently silent when vengeance and insults touched him alone, but who, in defence of his brother and others, could not restrain himself, but spoke out, and said what he would never have said for himself. Once in her life Barbara Petrovna was forced to hear the truth, and she heard that bitter truth from her favourite son.

Apparently Ivan Sergeyevich had avoided any hint about the previous evening; he had put up with many of his mother's questions, when she suddenly turned to him and asked, point blank:—

" Tell me, Jean, why last night, when I gave you such

a present, you didn't even want to thank me."

Ivan Sergeyevich did not reply.

" Really, are you again dissatisfied with me? "

" Listen, mamma," began Ivan Sergeyevich at last, " let us leave this conversation. Ah . . . why do you want to renew it? "

" And why do you not want to speak out? "

" Mamma, once more, I beg you, let us leave it . . . I know how to be silent, but I cannot lie and pretend . . . do what you will, I cannot . . . do not force me to speak . . . it is too distressing."

" I don't know what you mean by distressing," continued Barbara Petrovna harshly, " but I am offended. I do everything for you . . . you are dissatisfied with me! "

" Do not do anything for us. We don't ask you for anything now . . . please leave it alone, we shall live as we have lived. . . ."

" Not as you have lived! You have some property now," Barbara Petrovna continued to urge severely.

" Now why, tell me why do you say such a thing? " At last Ivan Sergeyevich lost patience. " We had nothing yesterday and we have nothing today, and you very well know it! "

" What, nothing! " cried Barbara Petrovna. " Your brother has a house and an estate, and you have an estate."

" A house! And you know that my brother is too honest to look upon that house as his own. He cannot fulfil the conditions on which you gave it to him. You demand that he shall live in it, but you won't give him anything to live on. He has nothing."

" What! He has an estate."

" He has no such thing! You haven't given us anything, and you won't. Your deeds of gift, as you call them, are not valid ; you can take from us tomorrow what

you have given us today.... Yes, and why all this bother?
The estates are yours. Everything is yours. Simply tell
us that you don't want to give us anything, and you
will not hear a word from us. But why this farce? "

"You are mad! " cried Barbara Petrovna. " You forget to whom you are speaking! "

" But I didn't want to speak. I wanted to be silent....
Do you think it was easy for me to say this? I asked
you to leave it," and there was such distress in his voice
that it seemed as if tears were choking him.

"I am sorry for my brother," he continued after a
short silence. " Why have you ruined him? You allowed
him to marry, compelled him to give up the service and
remove here with his family. . . . Before this he did live,
he lived by his own labour, he didn't ask you for anything, and he was comparatively comfortable . . . but
here, from the day of his arrival, you have doomed him
to misery, you are always tormenting him with one thing
or another."

"How, tell me how? " Barbara Petrovna was excited.

" In every way." Ivan Sergeyevich was in despair, and
could not help shouting. " Do you not tyrannize over
everybody? Who can breathe freely near you? " and
he strode up and down the room. " I feel that I ought
not to say this.... I beg you, let us stop! "

" So that is your gratitude for all . . ."

" Again, mamma, again you will not understand that
we are not children, and that your behaviour is insulting!
You are afraid of giving us anything! You think that
it would lessen your power over us! We have always
been dutiful sons, but you have no faith in us! Yes,
and you have no faith in anything or anybody. . . . You
believe only in your own power! And what has it given
you? The right to tyrannize over everybody! "

" So you think that I am wicked? "

"You are not wicked, but I do not know what is going on in your mind, why you should act in this way. Examine yourself, and remember what you have done."

"What, exactly? To whom have I done wrong?"

"To whom? Who is happy with you? Remember only Polyakov, Agatha . . . all whom you persecute, exile, they would all love you, all be ready to lay down their lives for you, if . . . and you make them all miserable . . . yes, and I myself would give half my life if I did not know all this, and had not to say it. They are all afraid of you, and they could love you. . . ."

"Nobody loves me! Nobody ever has loved me! Even my children are against me!"

"Do not say that, mamma, we are all ready, your children first of all. . . ."

"I haven't any children!" suddenly shouted Barbara Petrovna. "Go away!"

"Mamma!" Ivan Sergeyevich ran to her.

"Go!" repeated Barbara Petrovna still more loudly, and with this word she went out herself, slamming the door after her.

Passing through the hall Ivan Sergeyevich saw me; I was trying with my handkerchief to stifle the cries and sobs that were ready to burst out; he laid his hand on my shoulder.

"Don't, you will be ill again! What shall we do? I cannot . . ." and tears ran down his cheeks.

In a few seconds I saw him from the window; he was going down the lane in the direction of his brother's house.

I can see his tall, well-built figure before my eyes now. No-one, seeing him at that moment, could have had the least doubt that he was a profoundly unhappy man, for his walk and bearing expressed complete unconsciousness of anything around him. He walked with his head down, as if crushed under the weight of an endless, hopeless sorrow.

But it was not easy for Barbara Petrovna either. She only controlled herself until her son had gone. One can imagine what an effect his words had on her.

She had an attack of nerves. For a long time she could not be calmed ; there was no-one with her except Porphyry and Mme. Medvyedeva. Also it is easy to understand what happened in the house. It was such an awful day, that I couldn't think about anything except the dreadful scene in the morning. I went over in my mind all that I had heard. In my ears rang Ivan Sergeyevich's words, and Barbara Petrovna's broken sentences. Many years have passed, but I have forgotten nothing.

In the evening mamma sent for me.

" Go there! " . . . and at my perplexed and dumb question, she repeated impatiently. " There, there! Order the horses! "

I went to Nicholas Sergeyevich's. For what? Why? I don't know myself.

The first thing that met my eyes in the Prechistinska house was that everywhere were set out boxes, trunks and bags, giving evidence of preparations for a journey ; they were packing up to go to Turgenevo.

Nicholas Sergeyevich was in his study writing. Ivan Sergeyevich was walking backwards and forwards up and down the room.

I went in, threw myself on the first chair available, and wept bitterly. Ivan Sergeyevich brought me some water.

When I was a little calmer, the first to speak was Nicholas Sergeyevich.

" Did mamma send you? "

" Yes."

" Did she tell you what to say? "

" No, she told me to come here. I don't know why.
What shall I tell her? "

Nicholas Sergeyevich, with a look of despair, clutched
his head.

" The truth! We must tell the truth! " put in Ivan
Sergeyevich, sharply. " Say that we are getting ready
to go to Turgenevo, and that we are going tomorrow."

I flatly refused to take the message.

" Tell mamma," began Nicholas Sergeyevich, " that
I beg of her to read this letter," and he pointed to the
blank sheet of paper lying on the table. " I will send
her this letter tomorrow morning ; she is too much upset
today. I do not want to bother her."

" How is mamma? " asked Ivan Sergeyevich.

I told him all that had happened.

Ivan Sergeyevich listened to me, standing by the window and leaning his head on the glass . . . I could not
see his face, but I saw that he raised his handkerchief
to his eyes.

" I will come tomorrow," said he without turning
round.

I went away and told Barbara Petrovna about the
letter, and Nicholas Sergeyevich's request, and awaited
her inquiries, feeling like death. But she waved her hand
for me to go.

The next morning Nicholas Sergeyevich's letter was
given to her. We all knew the contents of this letter.
He wrote that he was going to Turgenevo with his
brother, with the intention of taking possession of their
father's estate ; he assured his mother of his love, and
his readiness to serve her, and begged her to forgive him
for this step which he was obliged to take, to support himself and his family.

Ivan Sergeyevich came himself.

Barbara Petrovna's sons never dared to go to her

without being announced. I knocked at the door.

"Come in," was the answer.

"Jean is here, mamma. May he come in?"

Then, instead of answering, Barbara Petrovna went to her writing table, seized Ivan Sergeyevich's youthful portrait, and threw it on the floor. The glass was smashed to pieces, and the portrait flew against the opposite wall.

When the maid came in and wanted to pick it up, Barbara Petrovna cried, "Leave it," and so the portrait lay there from the beginning of June to the beginning of September.

She would not see Ivan Sergeyevich, and he, having collected some of his things from upstairs, ordered them to be taken to his brother's at the Prechistenska house.

He made still another attempt to see his mother, but on receiving a refusal, went away.

I accompanied him to the porch. He said good-bye to me.

"I could not . . . what could I do?" were his last words to me, expressive of his regret for the scene of the previous evening.

The following day at twelve o'clock, I was ordered to go "there," and I understood without any difficulty what that meant.

When I arrived at the Prechistenska house, the gate was shut. The coachman who was still there came out of the house, and explained that the young masters had gone that morning by coach on the way to Tula.

Such days are hard to live through! Even now I feel that terrible inner trembling that I experienced then, as I went to Barbara Petrovna with the news of her sons' departure.

"What, they have gone?" . . . It seemed as if she couldn't believe it.

I had to repeat it. Then followed a scene that baffles description. A fit of frenzy overcame Barbara Petrovna. She laughed, wept, said a few disconnected words, embraced me and cried:—

"You alone now! You alone! I have no-one but you!"

There was no-one in the room with her except me. I was terrified and called:—

"Madame Schröder, Madame Schröder!"

Madame Schröder ran in.

Instantly Barbara Petrovna became calm, looked severely at her, and in a repressive voice said:—

"Go away!"

We were left alone again.

"How dare you call strangers when your mother is nearly mad?" she cried sternly.

But the interrupted attack was not renewed. I continued to stand there, hands and feet trembling, and ready to fall. At a sign from Barbara Petrovna I gave her a glass of water. The glass fell from her hand, and the water was spilled on her dressing gown.

She rang.

"Wipe it up," she said when the maid came.

"What time is it?" she asked in a quite calm, firm voice.

It was about two o'clock. Barbara Petrovna ordered Madame Medvyedeva to be sent for.

"Sasha!" Barbara Petrovna spoke with several pauses. "Go to Andrew, and tell him to get everything ready that we shall need in the country. We are going to Spasskoye. You, Barbara and Porphyry will go with me in the carriage, with post horses. Madame Schröder and all the rest will follow afterwards by coach. I want to take only what is necessary for me and Barbie, one carriage trunk."

And with these last words all was quiet. Not one
word, except curt orders, did Barbara Petrovna say during the following days. We all spoke in whispers, or we
even made signs.

The big carriage trunk was carried into the dressing
room. The maid tried to open the cupboards noiselessly, and move the boxes away from the drawers, from
which she took out the dresses and linen to be packed up.
And so that she would not make a noise with the keys,
she wrapped them in a handkerchief, and very carefully
turned them in the locks, because every sound was particularly irritating to Barbara Petrovna when she was
either ill or upset.

At such times she generally called out sternly:—

"I hear keys!" Or: "I hear plates and spoons!"
And then all was silent. People (that is, the servants)
moved about like shadows.

On days of this kind in our house I even managed,
with the elasticity natural to childhod and youth, to see
the cheerful or funny side of everything; but this time
all this stillness assumed such a sad, sombre tinge, that
it actually seemed as if someone, or rather something,
had died in the house.

We all recognised that this time we were not subjected
to any caprice or whim of Barbara Petrovna, that it was
not her power that was crushing us, but that she herself was bowed down under the weight of circumstances
for which she alone was responsible.

Chapter Fifteen

DEATH OF BARBARA PETROVNA

In a few days we went to Spasskoye.

Polyakov and his wife met us in the porch of the Spasskoye house. They had spent the whole year in the country, he for business reasons, and his wife on account of illness. Agashenka looked at her mistress in fear and sorrow (such was her devotion). This was not Barbara Petrovna! Why such a change? What was the cause of it? She could not imagine; nevertheless, her faithful heart was grievously affected by it.

She was sorry for her mistress!

When I told Agatha what had happened in Moscow, all that she said was:—

" Well, now there will be trouble for us all! "

But things were just the same at Spasskoye. The same quiet, the same silence, and only monosyllabic words and orders from Barbara Petrovna.

Three or four days went by, and I was allowed to ride on horseback, for the purpose of visiting the old people in Petrovsky.

I went into Barbara Petrovna's room, ready dressed, and with my riding whip in my hand. I found her terribly angry. Polyakov stood before her, pale, and with trembling lips.

Barbara Petrovna had heard, probably from some gardener's boy not familiar with the family drama, that the day before our arrival at Spasskoye, the young master and mistress (Anna Yakovlevna) had been to Spasskoye, and gone all over the house, gardens, greenhouses and forcing houses.

Actually, Nicholas and Ivan, foreseeing that in the

present circumstances they would be forbidden entry into Spasskoye, took advantage of their mother's absence to go and see their own den.

"How dare you let them come here!" Barbara Petrovna shouted at Polyakov.

"I did not dare to refuse, madame," replied Polyakov quite firmly. "They are our masters."

"Masters! Masters! I am the only mistress you've got!" and with these words, she tore the riding whip out of my hands and slashed Polyakov across the face.

This was Barbara Petrovna's last fit of anger.

From that day her health failed. The dropsy made swift progress. Her asthma increased, and, in the morning, the swelling of her face and round her eyes was more noticeable.

Day after day went by monotonously, and our life was far from cheerful. Barbara Petrovna, however, did not show any anger, nor did she persecute anyone. It seemed as if her power failed with her physical strength. Now she never manifested any harshness.

Her sons lived at Turgenevo, nine or ten miles away ; they wrote to her, but never got an answer. Ivan Sergeyevich sometimes came in secret to inquire about his mother's health, but I did not see him even once.

Porphyry gave decreasing hope of any improvement in his mistress's health. He was specially anxious about Barbara Petrovna's breathing; it showed the presence of dropsy on the chest. He began to talk about returning to Moscow, where he could have Theodore Ivanovich Inozemtsev's advice and help with regard to her treatment.

One morning, Barbara Petrovna felt very ill. In a few hours, she got ready and went to Moscow, taking with her only the doctor and Mme. Medvyedeva. She even left me behind at Spasskoye, and ordered Mme. Schröder and me to follow her, as soon as everything was arranged and in order.

Two days after her departure, in the evening about eleven o'clock, I heard a knock on the glass of the balcony door. Madame Schröder was frightened, and called to me not to open it; but I went to the door and opened it; before me stood Ivan Sergeyevich, wet through, straight from hunting, with his gun and game bag.

"How is mamma? How is her health?" were his first words. "I heard that she was very ill. Is she in danger?"

I set his mind at rest about that; said the danger was not yet specially imminent, and that Porphyry Timofeyevich had not expressed any fear of a sudden end.

Ivan Sergeyevich went into the hall, where one single tallow candle was burning in a copper candlestick. Our economical Michael Philipovich considered that one candle in the hall was quite enough for the young lady and madame (that is, Mme. Schröder), and obstinately insisted upon it, in spite of our demands.

We had finished supper earlier, and the table was laid for Ivan Sergeyevich alone. He asked us to sit near him and tell him how we were getting on, and how we had spent the summer.

There was nothing to tell. Ivan Sergeyevich was dull and preoccupied. I was not cheerful myself; my separation from Barbara Petrovna, who was ill, grieved me. The conversation flagged. The flickering candle made the room still darker, and the darkness was very much like this meeting with Ivan Sergeyevich; neither joy at meeting nor hope of anything better in the future. All this has remained in my memory like a kind of dull stain.

"I shall go to Moscow soon, and try again to get in touch with mamma," said he, on saying good-bye to me before going into his wing.

At last, Mme. Schröder, seeing that it would be awkward for him to talk in her presence about the most intimate side of his relations with his mother, left us alone.

"What does mamma do with our letters?" he asked in an undertone.

"She reads them," I replied.

"I am terribly grieved. It is a continual torture to me that I did not control myself then, and that I said all that I did," he continued quietly. "It would have been better to be silent to the end...Good-bye!" and he went out quickly.

The day of my departure for Moscow arrived. I left Spasskoye, and it never even entered my head that I had seen it for the last time. On arriving at Moscow, I found that Inozemtsev considered Barbara Petrovna's condition hopeless. To dropsy was added consumption, and the most complete loss of appetite. She lived exclusively on grapes, and later, on fruit ice-cream. Whether this was her own choice or the doctor's, I cannot say.

I know only that this lasted for nearly two months, and that Inozemtsev spoke very enthusiastically about the unusual strength of her constitution, and of her remarkable nature, which could live and think so sanely with so little support, at the age of seventy. But he sat for whole hours by Barbara Petrovna's bed, and, in conversation with her, never noticed the time.

But Barbara Petrovna felt the approach of death, and she often spoke to me about it.

Her mood changed perceptibly though not enough to

make a striking contrast to her former character. There were no more whims, or rebukes or anger; but there was neither gentleness nor humility, nor any special tenderness. She became silent.

In general she spoke little with her household staff, and if she said or ordered anything, it was in such an even, low voice, that even my practised ear could not draw from it any conclusion as to the state of her mind.

Her former feeling for her favourite Ivan was expressed in the following manner; his portrait, which had been thrown down in a moment of anger, was picked up, and was placed again on a little table near her.

To the mahogany bed on which she died, a small shelf of the same kind of wood was joined lengthwise, and on it lay that well known box in the shape of a book, with the inscription: *Feuilles volantes*. On these loose leaves Barbara Petrovna wrote something in pencil every day.

Later, after her death, we read these sheets. It was a diary, or rather, a confession.

She never spoke of her sons during her illness, and we were afraid to begin. She was very anxious about me.

On a bill of exchange, in A. Yevstafyevich Ber's name, to be given to me on coming of age, by Barbara Petrovna's wish was added an endorsement in my name, by which I was to receive fifteen thousand roubles in silver from her heirs.

My little box with its copper lock and my name engraved on it was examined and set in order.

A complete and detailed copy of all that it contained was drawn up by Leon Ivanovich, and I kept the key.

The following letter was dictated to me:

" *My dear children Nicholas and Ivan, I call upon you, at my death, to give their freedom to Polyakov and all his family, and to give him one thousand roubles gratuity; also to give his freedom to my doctor Porphyry Timofeyevich, and five hundred roubles gratuity."* Signed by her hand: *"Your loving mother, Barbara Turgenev."*

When this letter was signed she gave it to me.

"Take care of this letter," said she, "and when I am dead, give it to them, and tell them that I want them to carry out my last wish."

On the 20th of October, Nicholas Sergeyevich, having been informed of his mother's approaching death, the time of which Inozemtsev had almost exactly foretold, came to Moscow with his family, to his Prechistensky house.

In spite of all our efforts to induce Barbara Petrovna to speak about her sons, she was obstinately silent.

On the morning of the 28th of October, I went as usual into Barbara Petrovna's bedroom, and having said "Good morning, mamma," aloud, although in a trembling voice, I added: "I congratulate you. Today is Jean's birthday."

"Is it really the 28th today?" she asked in a rather shaky voice, and she looked at the movable calendar hanging on the wall.

Suddenly her eyes filled with tears. . . . I seized her hand and covered it with tears and kisses; another minute and I should have spoken to her about her sons, who, in their letters, always expressed their wish to see her, but she suddenly drew her hand out of mine: "Go! Go! . . ." and with the handkerchief with which she was drying her eyes, she waved me to the door.

I dared not persist, and went out.

But several times a day, unknown to his mother, Nicholas Sergeyevich came to inquire about her health

His mother's anger tortured him inexpressibly. He quite sincerely regretted that he had given her any cause of complaint, although afterwards, when the bitter grief had died down, neither of them could, conscientiously, reproach himself in any way.

With regard to their mother, they were not guilty. Her diary shows this clearly when we read the lines which refer to her sons. Deep in her heart she cherished her love for them. To send for them would have meant to give in . . . and the blood of the Lutovinovs flowed in her!

It was evident that a cruel struggle was going on in her mind, and we found proof of that also in her diary, written before her death. Here I may be permitted to quote a few lines from it. This is what we read on one of the sheets of paper: —

"*My mother! My children! Forgive me! And You, Lord, forgive me also, for pride, that deadly sin, was always my sin!*"

For a long time we waited a convenient opportunity for telling Barbara Petrovna that her son Nicholas was in Moscow.

On the 4th of November, Nicholas's birthday, I again went into her in the morning, and after the words: "I congratulate you, mamma, it is Nicholas's birthday," at one gulp, without taking breath, I added: "Nicholas is in Moscow."

Barbara Petrovna looked at me with her still shining, expressive, beautiful eyes, just as if she wanted to say something, but quickly turned away, moved the little bottles standing on the shelf from place to place, looked at one of them very attentively for a long time, and said: —

"Read to me."

I picked up some kind of French novel, and with a slight tremble in my voice, began to read. But it tired her. I had read a few pages, when I heard: "That's enough!"

I do not remember the date, but four or five days before her death, she wanted to perform her duty as a Christian.

Our parish priest, Father Paul, was called in from the Church of the Assumption at Yuspenia on the Ostozhenka. Barbara Petrovna made her confession, and partook of Holy Communion.

Either the words of the priest had an effect upon her, or it was her own impulse, but the day before her death she suddenly said to me: "Nicholas Sergeyevich!" . . . and it was her old, stern, imperative voice that I heard.

Nicholas Sergeyevich soon arrived. He threw himself on his knees near his mother's bed.

She stretched out her hand, now very weak, embraced him, kissed him, and in a whisper said imploringly:—

"Vanya! Vanya!"

"I will send a messenger for him at once, mamma," replied her son.

There were no reproaches or explanations between mother and son. He sat in an armchair at her feet, and I on a stool, nearer to her.

Twice Barbara Petrovna laid her hand on my head.

"Don't forsake her!" she said to her son.

But her meeting with her favourite, Ivan Sergeyevich, was not fated to take place. Ivan Sergeyevich did not find his mother alive.

How did it happen? Why did it happen? It remains a puzzle to me; there was time enough to let him know that his mother had expressed a wish to see him, and to inform him of her approaching death. I heard this from Nicholas Sergeyevich.

When, in 1880, a few days before the Pushkin festival, I saw Ivan Sergeyevich for the last time, he bitterly regretted this: —

"It is a great grief to me, very great," said he to me, "that it so happened that I was not present at my mother's death, or at my brother's."

At eleven o'clock on the morning of her death, Barbara Petrovna sent for Anna Ivanovna Kiryevsky and her brother-in-law, Peter Nikolayevich Turgenev, and, in their presence, she expressed and signed her last wishes concerning me.

At eight o'clock in the evening, Porphyry Timofeyevich sent word to "that house," that the hour of Barbara Petrovna's death was near. Since morning her breathing had been louder and more intermittent.

Nicholas Sergeyevich arrived with his wife between eleven and twelve at night. He, his wife, and I, were sitting in the hall. Suddenly hasty steps were heard in the corridor.

"She is dying! The priest!" said someone.

Nicholas Sergeyevich and I rushed into the bedroom.

Barbara Petrovna looked at us ; but suddenly her eyes grew dim, and the agony began. The priest managed to read through the prayer for the dying, and Barbara Petrovna was no more.

This was at ten minutes to twelve on the 16th of November, 1850.

May her soul rest in peace!

I say again: other times, other manners.

When Agashenka wanted to know something about my reminiscences I went purposely to see her. Having listened to everything, even the stories of her own sufferings, the good old woman sighed.

"Yes," said she through her tears, "she caused me much grief. I suffered much from her, but all the same I loved her! She was a real lady!"

Yegoryevsk, 1884.   *V. Zhitova,*
                              née *Bogdanovich.*